THE LAST WORD

THE LAST WORD

By

JEROME CHASE
and
JAMES D. BONO

Boston
BRANDEN PRESS
Publishers

© Copyright, 1976, by Branden Press, Inc.
Library of Congress Catalog Card Number 76-11437
ISBN 0-8283-1668-6
Printed in the United States of America

CONTENTS

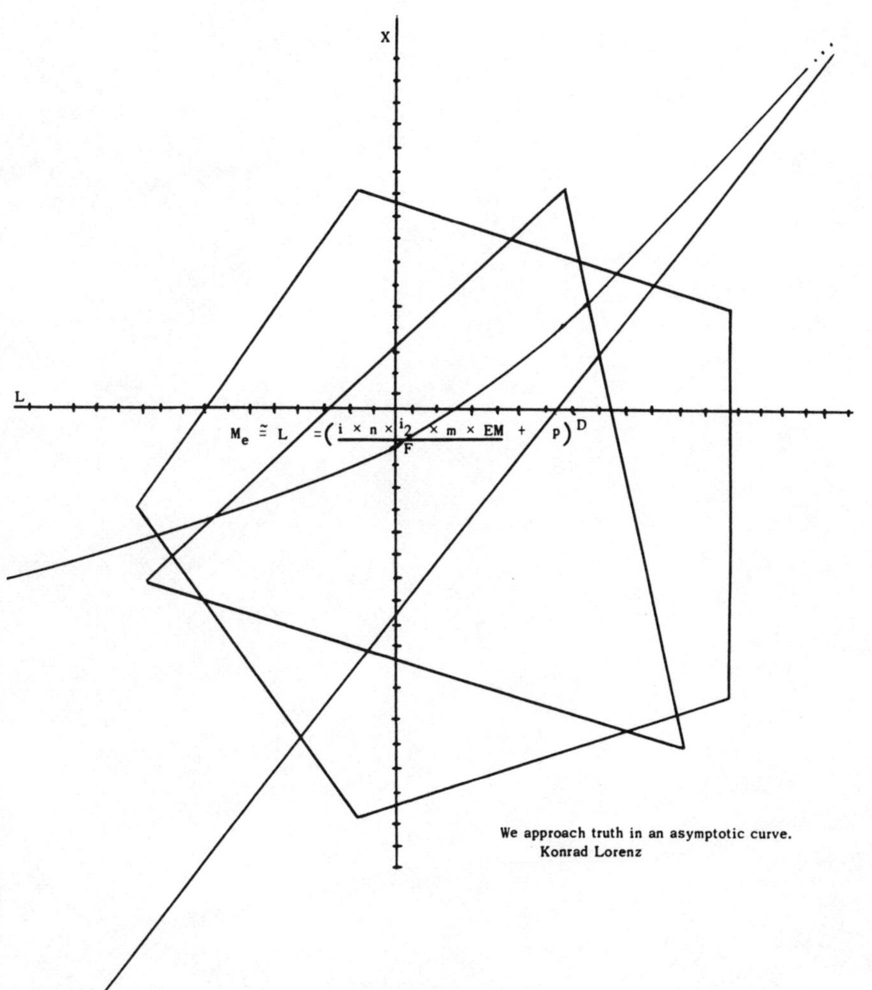

X
L
$M_e \cong L = \left(\dfrac{i \times n \times i_2 \times m \times EM}{F} + P \right)^D$
We approach truth in an asymptotic curve.
Konrad Lorenz

PREFACE

In January 1966, ten years ago, I assigned to a high-school English class the composition of essays on some controversial topic in the news, partially fulfilling, I thought, my profession's obligation to educate for good citizenship. A few weeks later Jerome Chase placed on my desk the twenty-eight page typescript which initiated an exchange unique in my experience as a teacher in several secondary schools, and as an instructor of foreign languages in two universities. For early in 1967, little less than one year later, Jerome presented as a term paper in world history a revision of the same essay, revised and expanded to answer my objections from the English course. He was sticking by his guns, and I found it necessary to warn him again of certain potentially serious errors.

Three years later, at Miami of Ohio in 1970, I was pleasantly surprised to find the name Jerome Chase on my enrollment sheet for first-semester Russian. As a term paper for this course I assigned the translation of an article of the student's choice from Russian to English. Mr. Chase this time proposed to update his essay of three years before, in order that he might include new material and respond to the critique I had written as his history teacher. Because he would not be translating, he promised to read a few historical texts in Russian and include them in his bibliography.

By now I was impressed and occasionally upset by the familiar ideas in his seventy-page theme on events still all too current, and was happy to make an end to the interchange by writing a careful commentary. But five years later, when I was teaching Scientific German at the University of Kansas, the story took on a new dimension. Now a graduate student in history, Jerome had continued to work on the book-length manuscript which had been a leitmotif of his undergraduate years. When I mentioned that Scientific German dealt with texts in the humanities as well as with the sciences, he resolved to enroll and challenged me to look at his work again. The latest revision contained an "essential" bibliography, and was accompanied by the proposal that if I would find a publisher, Jerome would do the necessary research and revision for a final version. Here it is.

I received permission to insert a few comments on the author and his philosophy as indications of our vehement disagreements, and further took advantage of the teacher's prerogative to speak the last word. People outside the educational system may find the results of our ten-year debate interesting. Jerome in my opinion pursues to their ultimate conclusion several ideas heatedly discussed in high schools and colleges today. My remarks are set off as here.

JAMES BONO

February 1976

FOREWORD

No man intentionally blinds himself.
— Gotthold Ephraim Lessing

On July 4, 1973, I completed what I felt was surely the final version of the paper to which my patient and esteemed teacher has referred. It was not by conscious decision that this high-school theme became the idée fixe of a long student career. No, the conviction that education today must not present a series of fragments, but a totality which should enable one with sufficient diligence to set down a precise, concise analysis of news events — that is what drove me. As I assembled bibliography through protest-marred presidential inaugurations, corresponded with authorities on Asian history, reworded and reformulated the arguments of this book, I began to perceive the complexity of ascertaining the truth from history books and newspapers, and soon stood in awe before the problem of stating it concisely. This awe is no doubt an unavoidable ingredient in the process of personal development termed "education".

There came then the signing of a peace settlement and intensification of combat and bombing in Cambodia and Laos. President Johnson died. No essay could strike the proper tone. When John Dean III concluded his testimony at Senate Watergate hearings, casting an incriminating cloud over the presidency, those events I had set out to elucidate seemed almost phantoms of a bygone age, buried in the past by inflation, under day-to-day and hour-by-hour developments in domestic affairs, and, on July 4, beneath tense speculation of reporters on the upcoming testimony of former Attorney General John Mitchell before Senator Ervin's committee. I started over again.

Where is the last word? Who dares to separate the essential from the non-essential in this disgorging cornucopia of news stories? Humbly or ambitiously, in writing or in private conversation, it is a task to be dared by everyone. Our news-magazine editorialists attempt to do so every week. Our schooling, our religion — it is each citizen's duty to approach the last word to the best of his ability, following his own asymptotic curve. Consequently, I think I may state without hubris what I set out to prove, a thesis which finds objections from all teachers and rebuttal from none, and which the benevolent reader will re-assess: Through all the confusion and detail emerge five of the most clear-cut and outlandish lies in history.

But how does one measure lies? Well, an untruth told about a trivial matter cannot be impressive, and obviously those un-truths are greater which succeed in deluding *many* people. Particularly when discussing subjects such as those enumerated above, it is important to distinguish between big and small lies. Taking the two functions as variables, then, I suggest as a pre-liminary formula for measuring lies, which we may alter subse-quently:

$$L = i \, x \, n$$

where i is the importance of the matter and n the number of people deceived. I think that a formula for measuring lies would go far toward establishing patterns among what are at first glance random and disconnected phenomena.

As for my dedication, I am beholden for this book to those who have engineered America's honorable peace. May the long view developed here provide a few handholds on precipitous terrain for the type of leadership which brought us through the Second Indochina War, in spite of great resistance at home and abroad, and in spite of the natural resistance accruing from some of the least equivocal, at once most obvious and deceiving lies — in a word, as Joseph Goebbels, author of the theory of the "big lie," would surely agree — from five of the greatest lies ever told.

Jerome Chase
February, 1976

PART I

At the same time that President Nixon took the oath of office on January 20, 1973, I reported for a school paper on the feelings of apprehension, futility, and anger apparent in both spectators and participants of a local demonstration, a small Kansas contribution to unwelcome nationwide criticism of the President's first-term policy. The timing of the last war protest incensed Nixon's supporters. As I sat before the bandstand in Lawrence, Kansas, listening to several censorious speeches, the gulf between community and protesters appeared unbridgeable, and newspaper coverage in the following days made it more so. Would any protestations to the contrary, however convincing, change a demonstrator's mind? For that matter, would these speeches alter a single opinion? *Must* communication present insurmountable obstacles? And *why* was polarization of opinion drawn along such bitter, permanent lines, with differences of opinion so vast? If no person intentionally blinds himself, why should it have been so impracticable to formulate a speech or compose an editorial which, rather than further inflaming already alienated opponents, might 1) foster communication and 2) summarize, on several crucial points of disagreement, conclusions of the many reliable books about Vietnam, written by authorities on Southeast Asian affairs? Such a synopsis might take the form of a five-part essay along the following lines.

1. Dissent

Certainly, citizens have modified their views over the years. Yet it is scarcely an exaggeration to say that they never changed sides in the Vietnam and related controversies. Some imprecise generalizing is necessary to make the point. Far more often Americans pledged allegiance to one group or the other and remained with that group, apparently impervious to arguments of others. Disagreement itself thus became a matter of paramount concern, a phenomenon as conspicuous among columnists and politicians as in the general public. Describe the disagreements of established columnists of ten years ago, and you outline their positions of today.

When has any great protest leader, from Jesus Christ to Mahatma Gandhi to Martin Luther King, expressed the opinion that one should exasperate one's ideological opponents? The Bible describes how to take an erring neighbor aside, first to consult with him alone — and then, if he remains intransigent, how to introduce a third party into the dispute, etc. Gandhi's emphasis on communication saved untold numbers of British and Indian lives and won his country's independence as well. Yet by every conceivable visual and verbal mannerism, dissenters divorced themselves from the majority in the United States.

2. Patriotism
Human kind cannot bear much reality.
— T. S. Eliot

In Kansas on January 20, many of the outraged onlookers' expressions could not be described as merely the critical glances protesters fear. One motorist, upon spying the procession, slammed on his brakes, clambered from his automobile, and cried, "Blow them off the face of the earth!" It was not possible to tell whether he meant this to apply to the protesters or the communists of North Vietnam.

How might journalists and other opinion-shapers have cleared the air? Perhaps by abandoning polemic and personal observation in order to concentrate on reviewing the definitive literature dealing with the history in question. Does bitter disagreement reign here also? Not at all, at least not on the five crucial issues of contention. A bibliographical essay (p. 37) defending this claim concludes my treatise.

2

Here I became impatient and could not resist jotting into the margin that I was quite skeptical of such a bibliography. If life has taught me anything, it has taught me that no subject can be found on which knowledgeable persons do not disagree. I feared it would cost Jerome Chase much to discover this for himself.

The scholarly Chase insisted with adolescent naïveté that someone must append a different kind of treatise to shelves of historical texts. Reading the same explications over and over became futile, he said. I brought out for his consideration the story of Procrustes, the mythical giant who so amusingly forced everything into a preconceived system.

I also had a few thoughts on dissent which may be worth inserting. When has any great protest leader, from Jesus Christ to Martin King, waged guerrilla war? Ho Chi Minh, an admirer of Mahatma Gandhi, cast about in foreign lands for thirty years (1911 – 1940), in France, America, and the Soviet Union, appealing for help to the principal negotiators at Versailles, later to capitalist and communist alike. But he returned to negotiate with the French from his own country, and finally opened hostilities himself six years later, in 1946. Here was an admirer of Mahatma Gandhi whose government killed, in what it later termed "a mistake," 15,000 peasants who opposed communist agriculture.

I am indeed interested in the writer who can present the "last word" on a life such as that of Ho Chi Minh. I concede that it is worthy of note that a Vietnamese communist was absent from his homeland for thirty years, during which time he petitioned the French in attempts to procure voting rights for Vietnamese in their own country, appealed to the United States in preference to Russia for military aid against the French, studied in Russia and rejected Stalinism on the grounds that it offered nothing but danger to small nations, calmed impatient militants from home, and so forth and so on. True, he resorted to guerrilla tactics only when betrayed by the French for the umpteenth time on March 6, 1946. But I want to see the college-age Thucydides who can explain such a life to the average American.

There are ironies about which the last word will never be stated — for example, that Vietnamese North and South, once prepared to embrace any great power, democratic or communist, which offered to help them toward independence from French institutions, ended by fighting each other. Disagreeing, liberals and conservatives, dissenters and VFW-style patriots will all find such ironies worth pondering; but Jerome Chase must also ponder the irony that Jesus Christ, Gandhi, and King were all murdered, while Ho Chi Minh died of old age, his country still divided by the

Geneva Conference of 1954, devasted by war, the dead numbering in seven figures and the living still largely controlled by outside influences. It cannot be the case that any man will put on paper the last word on the plight of small countries like Vietnam in the cold-war world.

Jerome read my story of Procrustes, but responded with another quote and the following "last word" on the few years of history to which he had been witness:

3. War

A systematic thinker might construct a great edifice on the subject of competition, ordering political machination and keeping-up-with-the-Joneses into a framework supported, say, by "the will to power" or "conspicuous consumption" as central concepts. To one insight into human behavior he could connect another and another. One could turn to philosophers or sociologists for explications of the intra-specific struggles in *Homo sapiens,* or one could turn to any number of religions. Or one could turn to comparative ethologists who study aggression in animals.

Which directions appear most likely to yield important answers we can better deliberate after a brief review of five startling misconceptions, in sections devoted to a) the origins and nature of conflict in Southeast Asia, and of similar conflicts around the world; b) government in Hanoi and Saigon, and in comparable capitals; c) the division of Vietnam in 1954, and the clash of ideologies in third-world countries; d) the deployment of weaponry by each of the armed camps in Vietnam, and around the world; and e) truthfulness in governments. The first three of these issues precluded peace agreements for years. The five together rendered the United States a house divided against itself once again. Each bears directly on the question how western nations can contain communism in poverty-stricken nations — that is, on the domino theory. Senate hearings on Watergate-related corruption did not raise more momentous issues than these five, but were in many ways born of these issues. Because none better serves to illustrate the validity of the domino theory, I wish to cover first the origins and nature of the Indochina War.

a) *Origins.* It is true that Eisenhower wrote in *Mandate for Change,* "I have never talked with a person knowledgeable in Indochinese affairs who did not agree that had elections been held as of the time of the fighting, possibly 80 percent of the population would have voted for the Communist Ho Chi Minh. . ." Some have taken Eisenhower's statement as the thread of Ariadne leading to an accurate assessment of the war's origins: it was a nationwide, indigenous revolt against a colonial power. Others have drawn quite the opposite conclusion. Kenneth L. Fox has recently editorialized: "There are people in this country who say that the South Vietnamese should have submitted to being taken over by Ho Chi Minh's forces in a stacked election 19 years ago." He concludes his editorial, "Ike Remark on Ho Election Put in Proper Context," with the words, "But that was for the South Vietnamese to decide. They chose to fight for the independence they now have lost as the darkness of Hanoi's domination settles over the whole of old French Indochina."
In the history books constituting my bibliography there is startling unanimity. United States administrations considered the undeniable popularity of Ho Chi Minh and decided to take the excruciating long view. America accepted responsibility for ensuring militarily some future chance at freedom for peoples of Southeast Asia, though such a chance presently remains denied them by military regimes. When freedoms guaranteed by the United States Bill of Rights fall before a communist system, they cannot be expected to reappear.
The United States government did not always place its moral and military support behind a carefully considered interpretation of the ultimate causes of the Vietnam Civil-War Revolution. Twenty-five years ago our State Department advised France to withdraw from Vietnam. Secretary of State George C. Marshall criticized the French strongly for siding with so many varieties of hatred-engendering social and political abuses: "We

fear the continuation of the conflict may jeopardize the position of all Western democratic powers in Southern Asia and lead to the very eventualities of which we are most apprehensive." He realized that the Indochina question was old when communism came to Russia in 1917, and held France partly responsible for the poverty and desperation in that part of the world. Two million Vietnamese had starved to death in famines caused by the plundering Japanese during World War II, which threw fuel on the flames. The American Office of Strategic Service collaborated with the Vietminh during World War II and delivered weapons to them in a common effort against Japanese expansionism, so that after the war Ho Chi Minh appealed to the United States for aid and support against the French return.

Few developments in the history of anti-colonialism reveal the nature of the conflict so clearly as this hope for American support among Vietnamese nationalists. Neumann-Hoditz explains why they saw Americans in quite a different light in those postwar years:

In the winter of 1944-45 Ho Chi Minh established his first contacts with the power which was to present a deadly threat to his country twenty years later. The Americans seemed to him. . .to be the only effective allies in the war against the Japanese and colonial rule. Unlike the French, English, and Dutch, the U.S. had no colonies and it had taken on the main burden of crushing the Japanese military machine.

George Marshall deplored the French return to Vietnam after World War II, which he saw as foolish, stubborn, and economically motivated resistance to the indigenous revolt. He supported the "legitimate desires of the Vietnamese." All this to me indicates the desirability of re-establishing and reaffirming the reasons why American diplomats led America into the same mess which had ensnared France.

I wish there were some simpler way of moving toward a formulation of the Great Lie. Perhaps Twain or Rogers or Friedrich Nietzsche could have found the way. At this point I can only state that one could hardly exaggerate the impor-

tance of a lie which so twists the origins and nature of a war
that fruitful public discussion of that war becomes a practical
impossibility. A precise formulation of the Great Lie must wait,
else this will sound like an editorial.

An irony which arose from the lie can be seen in the about-
face both French and Americans accomplished — for the French
it was quite a feat in doublethink indeed — after the 1954
Geneva Conference. At a news conference in 1964 de Gaulle,
who had insisted on the French return to Vietnam after the fall
of Japan in 1945 on the grounds that the "greatness" of France
required it, stated that the United States was now being ex-
tremely thoughtless in its Vietnam policy: "[The Vietnamese],
whatever their opinion of communism, are less and less inclined
to support a cause and an authority which in their view are in-
termingled with those of a foreign state." Accordingly, de
Gaulle declared assuredly, a military solution "cannot be expected." This 1964 conclusion was the very American counsel
he had refused to follow after 1946. His solution now was that
everyone should "return to what was agreed upon ten years ago
and, this time, comply with it." That involved, he explained,
two things:

The first is that the powers which directly or indirectly bear a responsibility in what
was or is the fate of Indochina — that is, France, China, the Soviet Union and America — be effectively resolved to be involved there no longer. The second is that massive
economic and technical aid be furnished to all of Indochina by the states which have
the means for it, in order that development replace cruel division.

Did de Gaulle expect China and the Soviet Union to withdraw from Vietnam? An unlikely exegesis. Ho Chi Minh was
as anxious to keep his country free from Japanese, Russians,
and Chinese as he was from French and Americans, and in that
regard he had been largely successful. What could have led to
de Gaulle's about-face? It must have been something basic and
concrete, such as that the modern world's mightiest movement
for national independence was about to come up against the

world's mightiest military machine. De Gaulle's statements amount to nothing less than an admission of French responsibility for decades of Vietnamese desperation by denying them voting rights, economic development beneficial to themselves, badly needed social reforms and educational opportunities of a national nature — responsibility, therefore, for a war which cost 174,000 French (and no one knows how many Vietnamese) casualties, and which drove the Vietnamese as a people into the iron curtain.

Will Rogers said that once ignorance gets started in a place, there is absolutely no stopping it. Ignorance had gained a very good foothold among the French, perhaps as solidly as it had among the English when American colonists sought independence from outsiders. Perhaps ignorance was present in France when the French government helped bring about the collapse of the Weimar Republic by draining Germany of iron, timber, and money in a time of worldwide depression. Soon a good man could not be heard.

But now I am wandering and must come to the point. I apologize to the reader that in ten years I have found no simpler way to state the last word than in these paragraphs. Before analyzing further, then, the language of the U.S. State Department or anyone else, let us simply call the child by his right name. The original error, now *the* Great Lie, indeed one of the greatest lies ever told and believed, one of the great cover-ups of history, is that the war before American interference should be characterized not as the end product of an anti-colonial movement with a centuries-long history (which it was), nor even as a civil war (which it also was), but as a war originating in a Russian and/or Chinese conspiracy, or some similar conspiracy, to conquer free nations. The Vietnamese had no interest in being dominated by a communist monolith. They either feared or hated their giant neighbors to the north. The one thing we could count on was their refusal to accept support, no matter how direly needed, from Russian or Chinese divisions on their soil, while Americans, Koreans, Australians were marching across the South in hundreds of thousands.

Why wage war against a people whose aim is independence from all great powers? In a brief summation of his book, Neumann-Hoditz gives us some idea of the French self-delusion:

Perhaps Ho Chi Minh would in fact have become a Vietnamese Gandhi, as some observers suggest, after the revolution was complete, if the French and then the Americans had not robbed him of the fruits of his victory. After gaining independence, he sought understanding and not violence. If the revolutionary youth of the West today identify Ho Chi Minh with violence, they are doing him a bitter injustice. And it was the misfortune of the politician Ho Chi Minh to be at one and the same time a nationalist and a Communist. The Americans therefore viewed him as their enemy once the cold war began.

Now I realize that the Vietnam War was a terribly complex affair, and leave it to the historians to state the last word about it. My aim is not to expound exhaustively on what the war *was*. To reveal as completely as humanly possible the course of a war is a long and arduous task. *Too* long. It is relatively simple to tell what a war was not. By 1954 certain politicians were making a name for themselves as our foremost patriots by assuring Americans that they had the last word on foreign policy. Without them and their lies, an independent, possibly even non-aligned Vietnam may have stood at peace as a great wall facing China. The Chinese may have known better than to attack the badger at their doorstep. Instead, to use Twain's imagery, a seed of lying was planted. It took firm root during the McCarthy hearings. And it grew.

The above differs little in import from Jerome's first attempt of 1966, at which time I was of course worried about the implications for the writer. Whoever has struggled to this height easily loses his equilibrium and falls on one side of the tightrope or the other — that is, into a dogmatic monism of some sort. It would scarcely be counted a wonder if a loyal citizen, having distilled the above exposition from historical studies, would first question his own sanity, then backtrack to reconsider his government's position. To appreciate the razor edge of polarization, one must pit expositions of the Great Lie against the long view of three United States presidents. According to the long view, the United States was attempting to maintain a foothold for freedom in Southeast Asia against international communism. One might naturally conclude that either the war originated as a revolt of the Vietnamese against a colonial power, or in the Soviet Union or China; and who was one to believe? A citizen might be excused for believing his leaders. How could Ho Chi Minh have been an admirer of the United States Constitution, an admirer of Mahatma Gandhi, and a minor Stalin? According to historical analyses, our administrations stated incorrectly, in self-contradiction, that American soldiers were fighting against Russian or Chinese aggression. American soldiers faced guerrillas already fighting against foreign interference. There is a great danger in bitterness and one-sidedness here.

Which brings me back to my main objection to this "last word" business. The world is complex and unpredictable, not simple. I want no part of any dogmatic monism. Perhaps one cannot resolve the controversy by restricting oneself to the origins of the war. There were issues greater than the destiny of Vietnam. If Southeast Asia fell to revolutions, what area of the world would be next? The world is replete with such tinderboxes. One-third of the world's population, we are told so often, is either malnourished or actually starving.

The trend of Jerome's argument might be reversed on the grounds that the survival of democratic institutions anywhere on earth is at stake. That would allow one to uphold some confidence in the depth of thought of American leadership, whether knowledgeable persons disagree on the Great Lie or stand as one man.

While knowledgeable persons do not disagree that we have been told the Great Lie, they do disagree with respect to the importance of the lie, and to its role in shaping the present. This indicates the necessity of adding a third variable to our formula for measuring lies. A lie which deceives a society's most intelligent people is greater than one which takes in only the unlettered. It is not necessary actually to *fool* the experts. If a liar out for personal gain can involve important, respected, and intelligent people in futile and endless debate, smug in his confidence that no final word will stand uncontradicted, the liar's purpose is served. While society's opinion-shapers spend time arguing whether he is telling the truth or not, how much of the truth he might be telling, and whether his lying is actually harmful, the liar can proceed to have things his way.

Our altered formula for measuring the greatest lies in history now reads:

$$L = i \times n \times i_2$$

where i is the importance of the matter, n the number of people deceived and i_2 the number of educated people deceived or made to appear dull-witted by the liar.

At one time it had been a sign of
madness to believe that the earth
goes round the sun; today, to believe
that the past is unalterable.
— George Orwell, 1984

b) *The Two Camps.* The second Great Lie deals with our worst foreign policy problem, and tells a great deal about the Cold War. It concerns the falsehood that the series of governments we supported in Saigon were benevolent dictatorships, or even governments something like our own — well, at least governments respectful of human dignity in some degree. . . or at least preferable to governments of the North. . . then again, perhaps Saigon would have been preferable to the North some day. You see, if one knows a little about the history of Saigon, it is impossible even to formulate this lie without backing down from it.

Peoples of most nations chafe, ignorant and malnourished, against the harness of corrupt social structures in such dystopias as North and South Vietnam — whose people, were they to have received all the practical benefits of energy and financing devoted to the military efforts expended there, would have enjoyed the highest per capita income in the world. One would be very arrogant indeed to say that one had the key to the problem of dealing with undemocratic allies. But it is not possible to live with any degree of peace of mind while one's government squanders money to commit future massacres in behalf of what may be the *worse* of two evils. Neither need one be particularly wise to see that Americans were sheltered from details of Saigon's confinement of men, including legislators, on trumped-up charges — often because the individuals concerned voiced a desire to negotiate seriously with the North. Any person with some measure of worldly wisdom knew that the Saigon government, itself the miscarriage of a wartime calamity, did not merely deal in corruption, but that its lifeblood was corruption based on the grabbing of American military aid. William Crum was not the only opportunist to note that millions of dollars were now in the offing.

For every American POW released by the North, over 100 enemies of Saigon remained in prisons in the South, where American reporters were forbidden to go and almost never went. Saigon insisted in its last year of power that it held only 27,000 prisoners. The American press reported that the total number ran to at least twice that. According to the humanitarian organization *Amnesty,* the three countries in which a citizen was most likely to be tortured by his government because of his political views were Brazil, the Soviet Union, and *South* Vietnam. The most cautious sources stated that somewhere between sixty and one hundred thousand people languished in concentration camps in South Vietnam. Very well, the American war supporter felt that these captives were instruments of the international communist conspiracy.

If they were, what brought that about? It may not be possible to state how our government should deal with undemocratic allies. A child could prove, however, that government in Saigon was in no way benevolent, American, or democratic. A high-school student might well feel confident in saying that his leaders were lying to him. He would not see it as an isolated incident when an appointed police chief raised his gun in Saigon and executed an untried man. He would see that as the tip of an iceberg.

A writer might help to alleviate the strains of polarization in America by most crassly and precisely pointing out the bones of contention, but not this way. In search of an explanation for the bitterness of polarization in America, a writer arrives perforce at the second Great Lie, the one defending government in Saigon as benevolent. He has no choice but to deal with it. He does not become bitter himself. You must begin differently, for people are satiated with paragraphs like the above. The worst has happened, again and again. It has no power to shock or to persuade.

My teacher has always known how to call me down and off at the proper time, for which I shall ever be in his debt. Alexander Solzhenitsyn himself claims he could not describe the sufferings of suspected sympathizers rounded up in South Vietnam and confined, without writ of habeas corpus, under conditions which met none of the rules of humanity agreed upon internationally. Our POW's were treated to a fine time by comparison. Men released by Saigon from Con Son were crippled for life after surviving humiliations best left to the imagination.

The question, "What audience might I reach?" overshadows all else in writing today. How many faculty members of service academies assign the reading of the *Bulletin of Concerned Asian Scholars* to their classes? Is it possible that no one but concerned Asian scholars reads the *Bulletin of Concerned Asian Scholars*? What percentage of West Pointers staunchly opposed the war? What percentage of a typical university faculty? Each of the polarized groups reads its own books — this group, *Masters of Deceit*; that group, *Slaughterhouse Five* — admires its own heroes — this group, Douglas MacArthur; that group, Samuel Clemens — and subscribes to its own magazines and newspapers. One nationally syndicated columnist justified bombing of Cambodia in 1973, reasoning that the United States "must maintain the credibility of its peace-keeping function" in Southeast Asia. The problem, he said, was basically "North Vietnamese Mickey Mouse." He gained a large audience for his views. Cadets and hardhats probably heeded him.

I have quoted Will Rogers, Mark Twain, Nietzsche, Orwell, and other men whom I consider "wise" — a word in need of definition. A wise man is one so familiar with the ways of the human animal, of leaders and followers of all walks of life, with governments and their methods, that he discerns patterns. The confusion of contemporaries does not surprise him. The debating of journalists does not confuse him. The sea of distractions does not seduce him. Saigon's treatment of political prisoners is only one of the many indicators a perceptive person could easily gather. For such an observer of humanity as Mark Twain, the first two Great Lies are conclusively underpinned by hundreds of details, so that in the end they operate like the jaws of a vise. If a government incarcerates legislators, closes down critical presses, is surrounded by racketeers, holds tens of thousands of politically suspect, rebellious citizens under inhumane conditions, and lies about all these activities — after the population has fought a war to eliminate these abuses — will it then win support of the people through Vietnamization? A man of the order of those quoted here recognizes signposts and regards journalists who lack a memory for them as "servants of the moment," neither interested in nor capable of appreciating the importance of a last word.

The world goes on as though it harbored an independent will, one conscious of a truth beyond human beings and contemptuous of their journalism. This cruel will has determined that after fighting so long *against* abuses which were very real, Vietnamese both North and South remain as far from representative government as ever.

The world teaches that one must also fight *for* specific and rather sophisticated governmental structures such as those attempting to right American government now through Senate hearings, that it is not enough to fight against things. Often a populace is not even in a position to fight *for* anything. Hans Fallada in his novel *Little Man—What Now?* (1932) portrays a national circumstance in which conditions become intolerable for the little man. The hero's life has for economic reasons reached a point where he has tried every means at his disposal to provide for his family, and now finds himself on the verge of a breakdown. His political choices are communism and fascism. He must choose.

Whatever the circumstances in Germany in 1932, this was the position of Vietnamese under the French and Americans. It was not that they could not make a choice. They had no choice. There was nothing to fight for, no movement of which either the American or the French citizen would approve. So many peoples today are in this position. The Vietnamese chose anyway, of course. They had to choose.

Any support of social abuses in the South unilaterally created additional reaction, in this case reaction in favor of the communist cause, the only alternative in a world which understands only power. Was the French military communism's best friend in Southeast Asia? The long view asks: In the long run, did the French possibly do more good than harm for the internationalist communist conspiracy in Southeast Asia? And in small nations elsewhere, which were watching?

It is peculiar to philosophy and politics that one argument and one lie never stand alone. An argument is as useful to the philosopher — a single lie, to the politician — as half a vise. If a philosopher presents one argument, he must present others to support it. More questions will arise, and in answering these the philosopher will discover still more questions; if a politician lies he must lie again and again, especially if his first lie was a big one. In the case of the United States in Vietnam, the first lie *was* a big one, and it had to give birth to another.

To aid in plugging in values for i, n, and i_2 of the formula, let us listen one more time to Neumann-Hoditz:

When the peace conference was convened in Versailles on January 18, 1919, the "modest demands of the Annamese people" were laid before the conference secretariat. They bore the signature Nguyen Ai Quoc [Ho Chi Minh]. On behalf of a "group of Annamese patriots" he had drafted these eight points with Phan Chu Trinh and Phan Van Truong, who translated the document into good French. On reading the text again today, one is astonished at how modest the claims of the Vietnamese patriots in fact were. They cover the following points: 1) A general amnesty for political detainees; 2) Equal rights for the Annamese and French in Indochina; 3) Freedom of the press and freedom of opinion; 4) Freedom to meet and assemble; 5) Freedom to emigrate and travel abroad; 6) Better school and educational facilities; 7) Abolition of the principle of rule by decrees of the French president rather than by laws; 8) Appointment of permanent representatives in the French parliament to support the interests of the Annamese.

There is no mention of independence or self-determination, even though the authors had been inspired by President Wilson's Fourteen Points. But Nguyen Ai Quoc [Ho Chi Minh] and his friends were to see their modest claims disregarded... Neither Wilson nor Lloyd George, let alone Clemenceau, received the insignificant and modest Asian.

... Was it surprising that Nguyen Ai Quoc and other patriots from many colonial countries welcomed the Bolshevik revolution in Russia and Communism in general as the beginning of their liberation? None of the established parties in the Western democracies seemed really interested in the colonial problem. The only promise of help came from revolutionary Russia and the Communists. How could it be refused?

Leading the American people in misunderstanding the Vietnamese conflict, American presidents have led them to misunderstanding of most of the world. For i in the formula we can insert, besides the war, "a twisted and false view of the whole world." For n we can plug in most of the people of the United States. For i_2 a value something on the order of "a healthy debate in which journalists bury the truth in tons of editorials." Apply the formula for measuring lies and you will see why America, as teachers and students in universities must poignantly perceive, is rent in half.

15

<blockquote>
They [the founding fathers] did not foresee
. . . the development of a vast communications
industry, concerned in the main neither with
the true nor the false, but with . . . non-stop
distractions.
— Aldous Huxley, *Brave New World Revisited*
</blockquote>

c) *International Agreements.* We must concern ourselves now not only with the true, but with the false. According to the long view, South Vietnamese requested the United States to aid them in defense of their country against an outside invasion. Here is John T. McAlister's analysis of what was to become the third Great Lie:

Although it stopped the First Indochina War, the partitioning of Vietnam by the Geneva Conference did not bring an end to revolution. While it separated the adversaries who had been locked in combat for seven years, this division of the country was intended to be only temporary, until elections could be conducted in 1956. But there were no binding international guarantees that these elections would in fact be carried out; nor was there any promise that the Vietnamese followers of the non-Communist State of Vietnam, who had withdrawn south of the 17th parallel, would participate in such elections or respect their results.

This lack of guarantees was in part a reflection of the inability of the conference participants to determine the exact purpose the elections were expected to serve. Article Seven of the Final Declaration of the Geneva Conference says that general elections "shall be held in July 1956," but it does not specify what issues were to be voted upon. Though this article calls for consultations to define the issues to be decided in elections, such meetings never occurred. These proposed elections were boycotted because the representatives of the State of Vietnam had, in effect, been excluded from the cease-fire negotiations in Geneva and their newly appointed Prime Minister, Ngo Dinh Diem, had denounced the cease-fire by proclaiming the date of their signing a national day of shame.

Despite the controversy over Diem's refusal to participate in general elections, it should have been clear that elections alone could not resolve the revolutionary conflict in Vietnam — particularly after the partitioning of the country. Since the future political order of Vietnam was what the seven years of war had been all about, it seemed most unlikely that the Vietnamese could simply stop fighting and settle their differences without the benefit of new institutions for sharing power and resolving conflict. But the creation of new institutions in which Communist and non-Communist might share political power and unite their country was regarded as an impossible task, especially during the emotional intensity of the Geneva Conference.

Because the conference participants did not wish to confront the complex dilemma of how a unified political order might be established in Vietnam, the great powers found a convenient substitute in proposing elections among Vietnamese on issues which were left unspecified. Although masked by a declaration of apparent consensus, the Geneva Conference participants only agreed on the points on which they disagreed, and thus they set the stage for a new phase of revolutionary war. – (*Vietnam: The Origins of Revolution*, Alfred Knopf. pp 341-3. Reprinted by permission of the Princeton Center of International Studies.)

What Mr. McAlister has stated in the precise but desiccated style of a Ph.D. dissertation could be stated differently and lose nothing in veracity. Doublethink must have begun on or around February 12, 1955, on which date the United States Military Advisory Group undertook the training of Ngo Dinh Diem's army. From that day on, over a year before the scheduled elections, Vietnam would be a growing dump for surplus United States military hardware.

It apparently did not occur to Secretaries of State Marshall and Dulles to refer to Vietnam as two countries. On the contrary, they insisted that Vietnam was one country, that the DMZ was a purely temporary arrangement, that the two adversaries were the French and the Vietnamese, and warned all against seeing the conflict in any other terms.

Books have been written to show how despised Diem was by most of his people, but reflection on his circumstance should indicate as much. Ngo Dinh Diem was a Catholic in a largely Buddhist culture, a French-speaking, French-supporting hangover from the French occupation. He recruited young men to fight against the North and their own neighbors so that he could establish a dynasty on American aid. He, not the majority of South Vietnamese, gave us a mandate to wage war over the heads of the civilian population.

The third lie, then, concerns the agreements of 1954 and runs counter to them in stating: 1) that Vietnam is historically two distinct countries, justly divided in the middle; 2) that the United States had a mandate from the Vietnamese people to maintain the division; and 3) that the United States had to maintain the division for security reasons – that is, to protect freedom, justice, and the American way from communist invaders. One can ignore this three-pronged chimera until the time comes to negotiate, whereupon the issues will be so basic that the shape of the negotiating table will present a problem.

What if the American public had suddenly realized that "under no circumstances," to quote Secretary Dulles, should the DMZ be regarded a political boundary? White House press releases such as the one dated July 23, 1954, had welcomed the resolution "prohibiting the introduction into Vietnam of foreign troops and military personnel as well as all kinds of arms and munition." In that press release dated July 23, two days after the signing of agreements at the Geneva Conference, Secretary Dulles expressed hope that the agreements would "permit Cambodia, Laos and Vietnam to be really sovereign and independent nations." In the heyday of Senator Joe McCarthy, Secretary Dulles was apprehensive neither of China nor the Russians, but of the French, whom he admonished: "Prime Minister Mendès-France said yesterday that instructions had been given to the French representatives in Vietnam to complete by July 30 precise projects for the transfers of authority which will give reality to the independence which France had promised."

So America had no choice but to support Ngo Dinh Diem's political vacuum, regardless of written agreements, long after Ngo Dinh Diem was dead, through coup after coup, general after general. Naïveté had characterized the discussions at Geneva anyway, since one could hardly have expected the Vietminh, who had won all in war, to about-face and tolerate the management of elections by its very war enemies, this time in affiliation with even more powerful outsiders. Now the country, we said, should be considered two separate states, and the nationwide insurgency an invasion of the South by a foreign state. And that it soon became. The United States had helped to create a situation in which the traditionally most brutal type of war, civil war, would be conducted under the most brutal conditions — over the heads of a civilian population, partly with sophisticated weaponry deployed by men who really knew nothing of the conflict and could not communicate with the populace, partly with whatever weapons fanatical nationalists — first nationalists, then communists — could beg, borrow or steal and drag with them through the jungles.

Will Rogers, Mark Twain, Nietzsche, Orwell, and Huxley are much admired for their low opinion of the critical faculties of their contemporaries. They describe the tendency of entire peoples to become blinded and lose their capacity to judge conclusive information though it flaunt itself all about them. Seldom do we pause to appreciate the specific, crass contrasts between truth and falsehood which, in a specific problem area, led those respected writers to their pessimistic view. Generally they resign themselves to the position that one cannot tell the truth straightforwardly in this world, so they write short stories, novels, and utopias. In this way they gain an audience, though a limited one, put forth views in disguised form and save themselves, at least from ridicule. And America, having failed to understand them, is upset *now* about Watergate.

The strident tone troubled me. Therefore I promised to aid Jerome only if he would allow me to insert these mitigating comments. How many times I tried to arouse sympathy and understanding in him for the attitudes of his compatriots. They had honestly believed that when Nixon came to the presidency he would attempt to end the war as soon as possible, to withdraw gradually, and turn the country over to the South Vietnamese government. These people were not lovers of war.

Also, laudable as his attempt at communication was through the last seven or eight years of war, my best student did not comprehend the futility of his effort. Any experienced teacher could have foreseen the problem: Generalizations preceding detail are meaningless to the inexperienced. Students cannot appreciate an idea no matter how clearly stated until the background has been laid. Even when they grasp the meaning of the individual words, perhaps even of the generalization itself in the abstract, the insight will not set with them as with one whose understanding rests on a great amount of detail.

I have often despaired of explaining the importance of democracy to youngsters raised in one. How to make clear the plight of Hungarians, Latvians, and others before the communist advance to a student who does not know where Hungary and Latvia are and who has no conception of European history! As a foreign language teacher I have known many Hungarians who gave up everything they owned in order to flee to an uncertain fate in Austria, and Latvians who exchanged their possessions for a flimsy skiff in order to set out into the Baltic to escape from the Russians. History is full of detail and strange language. The average high-school student considers the history text full of irrelevance and trivia. It is a good idea, a laudable undertaking, to present the conclusions of books before detail, but it will not work. Jerome will have to reach out for more and more detail to make his points, his essay will grow longer and longer, and he will be in the same boat with teachers, journalists, and historians everywhere. Truth is in the totality.

Although detail must precede generalization, peoples everywhere take the opposite approach. They jump to the conclusions they like, and there they stay. Man's thinking is simplistic, and may always be so. For Americans, it was the truth that the United States must contain communism in Vietnam. For many Asians, it was the truth that one must combat these grasping, arrogant outsiders. When American public opinion turned on the war, I think our leaders really tried to extricate themselves from it, and didn't know how. The North was stronger than we thought, and there were Tet and other major advances on their part, with the result that both Johnson and Nixon thought it necessary to use force and plenty of it, at the risk of bringing China and possibly Russia into the conflict. All the time they had to present their policy as generalizations designed for public consumption. Americans backed the President's foray into Cambodia and Laos on the basis of such generalizations, not knowing of the labyrinth of espionage and bribery which had rid these countries of opposition to such incursions.

Still, a high-school student comes up with ideas which defy Locke's dictum that there is nothing in the intellect which was not in the senses. You see what I mean — how startling and uncommonly persuasive Jerome can be, and he presented these very theses as a high-school junior. How many times have I been stung by marking a paper of his before knowing where he was headed, only to find myself forced by the profundity of an unforeseen argument to recant and write, "Never mind, Jerome, I see that. . ."—erasure of red ink being out of the question.

Every teacher must have suffered at some time the ill fortune of brusquely, impatiently overriding a pupil's thought, only to redden and apologize when the latter's intent dawns. In my profession one must learn to ride these blows as best one can — and above all to avoid them by reading the most slipshod papers before marking, and by giving attentive audience, without condescension, to inane classroom discussions.

To my mind Jerome Chase serves as an excellent spokesman for his generation, so I will take this opportunity to say a few words about him. As a lad he had a knack for bewildering us teachers. A congenial character as a rule, raised on a farm, an avid quail and pheasant hunter, he is by no means the scholarly type — taciturn, but with a bad daydreaming problem. Perhaps the experiences gathered from country life explain the early capacity to grasp certain aspects of the war. "Imagine putting an M-16 into the hands of a city-kid and sending him off to a hostile Asian village," he once said. He has the disconcerting habit of absently staring directly through a person, obviously not hearing a word. When roused back to the present and filled in on the topic at hand, he discovers his whereabouts and answers questions in an amiable manner.

A shock of hair which he attempts to smooth back falls above one eye, so that in spite of his shyness the penetrating stare strikes strangers as resembling the look of a certain mad tyrant. An utterly false impression, for his is a moralistic outlook on life, which made me fear early that he would grow up to be a bitter and intolerant person himself, one without appreciation for the inevitability of historical developments. The very sensitivity which aroused his indignation could easily result in loss of objectivity, which would be detrimental if he went ahead with plans to become a journalist. When such persons err they err greatly. So I gave him Dostoevski's *The Possessed,* Hoffer's *The True Believer,* and Günther Grass' *Local Anesthetic.* They made some impression, but into his little book of quotes went Brecht's "I ate my food between massacres; the shadow of murder lay upon my sleep."

Brecht so despised the capitalists of West Germany, whom he held as responsible for world war as the Nazis, that he became an apologist for a communist government. The great err greatly, I have often heard, and it is true.

None of my fears have thus far materialized. In person Jerome is a gentle, diligent soul. In the following pages he continues to develop what I admit, in spite of my negative last word, are many fine points connecting Vietnam and Watergate. The reader who believes he has him pegged should adopt the teacher's stance and wait.

The précis developed thus far has provided in the third crucial issue the third side of an equilateral triangle, which Buckminster Fuller has dubbed the strongest figure in nature. The United States violated the international peace agreements of 1954 almost immediately and most blatantly. Each side of the triangle thus formed is closely related and connected to the other two, has little meaning without them, encompasses an area clearly defined only with the aid of the others, and guards that area against irrelevance. No one can discuss a triangle unless it has all three sides.

The area of the triangle described by the first three Great Lies appears to contain an important message: The domino theory is valid. That is not a simple message, however. A complete understanding of it might entail a great deal of study. Experience might not suffice for one raised in relative comfort; a student might have to read the writings of all the men I have quoted and many more in order to understand such a domino theory.

Before the chain reaction can take place, dominoes must be placed in a row and set on end. It is very difficult to knock them down otherwise. Not impossible, but difficult. A political scientist could do worse than bring the domino theory into perfect focus.

Against Russia and China, the United States needs the strongest deterrent. America must shoulder the burden of producing weapons to discourage Moscow and Peking. A college dissident who does not appreciate this, after what has been learned from Hitler and Stalin, Hirohito, Mussolini and others, is a child.

But to place the domino theory in proper light it will be necessary to discard the pretty triangle and investigate a fourth great lie: the brutality of the enemy in Vietnam dwarfed our own brutality and that of the ARVN.

Oh Lord our God,
help us
to tear their soldiers
to bloody shreds
with our shells; . . .
help us
to lay waste
their humble homes
with a hurricane of fire . . .
—Mark Twain, "The War Prayer"

d) *Physical Force.* The Senate Subcommittee on Refugees informs us that in South Vietnam alone, from 1965 to 1972 alone, there occurred 1,350,000 civilian casualties. For every

American who died in Vietnam, according to that committee, nine South Vietnamese civilians were killed. Most of these were killed by shelling and bombing, the B-52 and the free-fire zone being the most lethal weapons. For every American killed in action, twenty-three enemy and ARVN soldiers lost their lives.

Many journalists did not mind their country's talk of restraint in weapons deployment, in spite of the presence on the bookshelves of such studies as Edward S. Herman's *Atrocities in Vietnam: Myths and Realities,* and John Gerassi's *North Vietnam: A Documentary.* Early in 1973, during some of the heaviest bombing, many journalists at last became angry — at those greeting Watergate revelations "with glee." They did not want to see Americans "lose confidence in their government."

Certainly, everyone realizes the power of modern weaponry. But it evidently does not mean much to those spared war for over a century. It means nothing to Americans that their navy, by its proud assertion, assaulted a foreign countryside for years with weapons capable of blasting away thirty-six feet of concrete. Would the American reaction to such bombardment of Ohio farmland, with more tonnage of explosives than was dropped in World War II, result in our confidence that the foreigners would set up a proper government for us? We assaulted more than farmland.

Some field of study should provide the answer to the question how these lies spread in America. At any rate, without the aid of certain journalists, Americans would not have assimilated the lies. One wrote, "Let's get it straight: Richard Nixon's resumption of the bombing is the logical, not the illogical, the honorable, not the dishonorable, consequence of the breakdown of the negotiations in Paris as the result of North Vietnamese Mickey Mouse." Now this matter has nothing to do with liberalism versus conservatism — and I have no idea why so many conservatives insisted that we hurt only the minimal number of civilians — but solely with human suffering.

It was not the M-16 in villages, nor naval guns, but the jet, the helicopter, and the howitzer which snuffed out hundreds of thousands of lives. Still, the following GI letter, one of many contained in John Gerassi's book and first printed in the *Akron Beacon-Journal,* shows how our military lied to us:

Today we went on a mission and I'm not very proud of myself, my friends, or my country. We burned every hut in sight!

It was a small rural network of villages and the people were *incredibly* poor. My unit burned and plundered their meagre possessions. Let me try to explain the situation to you.

The huts here are thatched palm leaves. Each one has a dried mud bunker inside. These bunkers are to *protect* the families. Kind of like air raid shelters.

My unit commanders, however, chose to think that these bunkers are offensive. So every hut we find that has a bunker, we are ordered to burn to the ground!

When the ten helicopters landed this morning, in the midst of these huts, and six men jumped out of each "chopper," we were firing the moment we hit the ground. We fired into all the huts we could. Then we got "on line" and swept the area.

It is then that we burn these huts and take all the men old enough to carry a weapon and the "choppers" come and get them (they take them to a collection point a few miles away for interrogation). The Viet Cong fill their minds with tales saying the GI's kill all their men.

So, everyone is crying, begging and praying that we don't separate them and take their husbands and fathers, sons and grandfathers. The women wail and moan.

Then they watch in terror as we burn their homes, personal possessions and food. Yes, we burn all rice and shoot all livestock.

Some of the guys are so careless! Today a buddy of mine called "Lai Dai" ("Come here") into a hut and an old man came out of the bomb shelter. My buddy told the old man to get away from the hut and since we have to move quickly on a sweep, just threw a hand grenade into the shelter.

As he pulled the pin the old man got excited and started jabbering and running toward my buddy and the hut. A GI, not understanding, stopped the old man with a football tackle just as my buddy threw the grenade into the shelter. (There is a four-second delay on a hand grenade.)

After he threw it, and was running for cover (during this four-second delay), we all heard a *baby* crying from inside the shelter!

There was nothing we could do. . .

After the explosion we found the mother, two children (ages about six and twelve, boy and girl) and an almost newborn baby. This is what the old man was trying to tell us!

The shelter was small and narrow. They were all huddled together. The three of us dragged the bodies onto the floor of the hut.

IT WAS HORRIBLE!!

The children's fragile bodies were torn apart, literally mutilated. We looked at each other and burned the hut.

The old man was just whimpering in disbelief outside the burning hut. We walked away and left him there.

My last look was: an old, old man in ragged, torn, dirty clothes on his knees outside the burning hut, praying to Buddha. His white hair was blowing in the wind and tears were rolling down. . . — Reprinted by permission of the *Akron Beacon-Journal.*

While they do not account for the dead killed by B-52's and shelling, letters of the GI's who took part in search-and-destroy missions for any length of time show how, by assenting to spread of the fourth lie, America was the second power to prepare Southeast Asia for communism. Watergate was a scandal? *This* is the scandal!

Have our media or our leaders shown any tendency to discuss the fact that the United States is presenting the world with what in many places may well be the worse of two evils? Let the American working man envision himself earning fifty cents an hour with no unions in existence, no educational opportunities or other promise for his children, his government corrupt beyond redemption, spending the country's wealth on modern weaponry and allowing a privileged aristocracy to make a killing by exporting the country's raw materials. Such are the conditions which lay countries open to the communist advance, and if we expect to defend dictators at the head of such countries with weapons alone, we may as well prepare ourselves for a long, costly, divisive, and bitter siege. In a poor world one also needs *moral* force.

Our government stated that we were fighting the sphere of Russian and Chinese ideology in Vietnam. How, then, do we explain Ho Chi Minh's refusal to accept the support of their armies? When militants asked that he invite Chinese personnel onto his soil, he replied, "I would rather smell French shit for five years than Chinese shit for the rest of my life." With that type of man I believe the United States could have found *some* common ground.

When Ho Chi Minh asked for aid from the West after World War II, as he had after World War I, he turned to the United States. He had seen the callousness of the Soviet Union toward smaller nations. He did not wish for his country the fate of nations stretching from Albania to Finland. Indeed, it is inconceivable why any small nation should wish that fate on itself. Ho Chi Minh never forgot the Stalin purges. As for China, he feared her as do all Vietnamese, and realized well that his country could be swallowed by China as it had been before.

All this is bad enough. But then the United States turned its military loose to wage war in Cambodia, Laos, and Vietnam, driving even Sihanouk into Chinese arms. Is it a wonder casualties were high? During our own Civil War we could not prevent camps such as that at Andersonville from springing up, where Union soldiers were beaten and starved, frozen and abandoned to disease by the thousands. We could not prevent a Sherman from slicing a broad swath of death and destruction across the countryside of his own former compatriots. You would expect this to tell newsmen something about restraint in Vietnam, would you not? There was more Shermanesque arrogance than restraint in the deployment of weaponry in Asia. Where is the mystery? In secrecy military policy was planned which took effect on the other side of the world. Soldiers were instructed to burn villages and shoot livestock in contested regions. Officers were supplied scorecards as incentives to up body counts for the sake of promotion.

Mark Twain spoke the last word about this, and perhaps even about the domino theory, when he wrote of American action in the Philippines:

I pray you to pause and consider. Against our traditions we are now entering upon an unjust and trivial war, a war against a helpless people, and for a base object — robbery. At first our citizens spoke out against this thing, by an impulse natural to their training. Today they have turned, and their voice is the other way. What caused the change? Merely a politician's trick — a high-sounding phrase, a blood-stirring phrase which turned their uncritical heads: *Our country, right or wrong!* An empty phrase, a silly phrase. It was shouted by every newspaper, it was thundered from the pulpit, the Superintendent of Public Instruction placarded it in every schoolhouse in the land, the War Department inscribed it upon the flag. And every man who failed to shout it or who was silent, was proclaimed a traitor — none but those others were patriots.

. . . This republic's life is not in peril. The nation has sold its honor for a phrase. It has swung itself loose from its safe anchorage and is drifting, its helm is in pirate hands. The stupid phrase needed help, and it got another one: Even if the war be wrong we are in it and must fight it out. We cannot retire from it without dishonor. Why, not even a burglar could have said it better. We cannot withdraw from this sordid raid because to grant peace to those little people on their terms — independence — would dishonor us.

Today the burglary is of a different sort, the Vietnam War enabling certain Americans to burglarize political headquarters and to pick the pockets of their compatriots with a clear conscience. Shakespeare had the last word for that, and would have seen that personal ambition and greed were in the last analysis the main causes of the Vietnam War.

The number 1,350,000 applies to South Vietnam only, from 1965 to 1972 only. It does not include North Vietnam, Laos, or Cambodia, where some of the most atrocious bombing raids, and least restrained, were carried out. Perhaps during the sixties the Southeast Asians came to hate and fear North Vietnamese and Americans equally. I don't consider it healthy to debate that now.

To return to the formula, it becomes more and more apparent that by nearly any measure our Great Lies vie with the most impressive of all time. Some explanation must be sought for the willingness of people to believe them. For aside from the importance of the matter and the people deceived, a lie deserves to be judged by its degree of falsehood. In other words, how monstrous is it? Is the matter so complex that one could not expect any but experts to judge? Or is it relatively simple?

Americans needed to believe that their shelling and bombing were not killing many civilians, but that, at least, is not a complex issue. Without a lie to reassure them, Americans could not have tolerated body counts week by week. Without the fourth lie, the first three would have begun to wobble like a three-legged card table. The magnitude (m) can be defined as the distance of the story told from the actual situation, leaving us with this formula for measuring lies:

$$L = i \times n \times i_2 \times m$$

Watergate did a great service. It disproved the fifth lie: that American government is basically truthful. This it did so convincingly that I believe Americans will now listen to a careful assessment of the domino theory, so that no Vietnam, no Chile, no Guatemala — no nation of poor, shall again be the cause of American crimes against humanity.

It has happened before.
Strong men put up a city and got
a nation together,
And paid singers to sing and women
to warble: We are the greatest city,
the greatest nation:
nothing like us ever was.
- Carl Sandburg

e) *Moral Force.* Of course Will Rogers was joking when he stated that communism is a good idea. He knew that it is not even good as an *idea*! Communism is a reaction of the embittered to other systems which fail. No people has ever adopted the communist system which had a good chance to reject it. Marx was reacting to child labor — children working over ten hours per day for pittance wages. Communism in Cuba, too, was a reaction, and in Vietnam. It prevails in these countries now not because communism won the hearts and minds of people, but because of the failure of previous capitalistic systems.

"The supreme tragic event of modern times is the murder of the six million Jews," writes Susan Sontag in *Against Interpretation.* "In a time which has not lacked in tragedies, this event most merits that unenviable honor — by reason of its magnitude, unity of theme, historical meaningfulness, and sheer opaqueness. For no one understands this event." How regrettable that so many prominent writers can come to such a conclusion. On the contrary, the causes of that catastrophe are clear: power-seeking by demagogues manipulating public opinion, concentration of economic power in unscrupulous hands, careerism to the exclusion of principle, use of technical devices to deprive ethnocentric, possibly instinctively motivated people of independent thought, the virtual philosophical and economic militarization of an entire nation — most people realize that these things each played a role in the complex story. To think that the killing of Jews was incomprehensible is to overlook dozens and dozens of lesser massacres. Since the Boer War political prison camps have been in existence somewhere in the world, and they exist now. Whether in Brazil, Siberia, or Southeast Asia, the fact that certain circumstances lead to the incarceration of thousands in horrendous camps is inescapable. The magnitude of these events is largely a matter of historical accident, depending on the type of leadership at the reins. Here we have ten thousand, there fifty thousand imprisoned for political reasons. Genocide is genocide whether practiced in Brazil, Germany, the Soviet Union, or Vietnam.

When we consider that in addition to such behavior ever greater numbers of humanity never rise above a nearly animal existence due to hunger, illiteracy, poverty, and overcrowding, then it becomes apparent that our age is by far the most wasteful of all. Camps in Siberia may have destroyed as many lives as those in Germany. If those in Siberia and Germany destroyed more numerically than those in Vietnam, that is not because of the wisdom of today's Americans, but because history would have it so. It is harmful to speak of Germany as of a sort of weird, unspeakable accident which no one understands, in an age when in India, Africa, and South America the extent of misery leaves only one consoling thought: each individual suffers and dies once.

Eisenhower saw that impersonal forces, a great deal of intellectual dishonesty, as well as unscrupulous individuals were at work in the industries and military circles dependent upon weapons contracts. His thinking justifies Mark Twain's scornful analysis of "man's descent from the higher animals." A certain brand of capitalism will sell out any cause, or support any, to achieve its ends. It will work children half to death for starvation wages. It has welded its names onto the ovens of Buchenwald for the world to see. Its cynicism knows no bounds. Much of the world is faced with the choice between this capitalism and communism, with no middle ground to stand on.

The causes of the catastrophe in Germany are numerous, but they are not unusual or incomprehensible. They do not differ in important respects from the causes of massacres in Brazil. One of the most important factors has much to do with the fifth and last lie to be discussed here: that the United States government is basically truthful.

The government twisted public opinion on the war, not on occasion but constantly for years. I know many kind-hearted people who supported the war in Southeast Asia. A few wished to drop a hydrogen bomb on Hanoi. More wished to exercise more restraint and merely level Hanoi and Haiphong conventionally. The majority wished to continue exercising more of the restraint already exercised while hoping for some diplomatic

solution. When I think of their kind-heartedness, I feel sorry for
having to write harsh sentences and turn to those who have misled them. It must have been a very untruthful government
which misguided my contemporaries to this extent.

It comes as no surprise that German writers have discussed at
length the subject of truth in government. In his trilogy, *The
Sleepwalkers* (1931), Hermann Broch attempts to analyze three
generations of German history. "How is this extent of adapta-
bility possible?" he asks. In giving his lengthy answer he explains the German desire for a strong leader, ". . . so that he
may provide us with a motivation for events that in his absence
we can only characterize as insane." The same can be said for
some of our leading journalists. There are many worlds and all
kinds of hell on earth besides the communist one, and a few
prominent individuals out of contact with them can attach the
appearance of normality to that which otherwise everyone
would term insane. One insane thing to which they attached as
much normalcy as possible was the body count.

The government deceived Americans about the most important aspects of foreign policy. There are many kinds of oppression to be dealt with. One type is the communist variety, which
regiments people onto collective farms and deprives them of
private property. There is also the dictatorial oppression of Papa
Doc Duvalier. There is economic oppression, which means being
pinned to one place, without choice or hope, in order to survive. There is the oppression of absentee landlordism, the oppression of having one's country occupied by untrustworthy foreigners, the oppression of being conscripted into an army to
fight for a government one does not support. There is the
oppression of not knowing when the bombs of one's protectors
will fall, or where. And there is the oppression of living in a
country systematically committing crimes against humanity and
being able to do nothing about it, indeed having to *pay* in
dollars for it, because one's government is lying and because
men without a trace of historical objectivity — irresponsible,
witty, narrow-minded, conceited, and verbose nincompoops,
foul the democratic debate.

Nietzsche reproached such sheltered individuals with, "If you
can't hit the nail on the head, don't hit it at all." Perhaps

Lincoln felt this way when he snapped to Harriet Beecher Stowe, "So *you're* the one who caused this great war." Not that *she* deserved the reproach.

Lincoln might have been speaking to journalists of today when he urged them to recognize the seriousness of their debate: "If there ever was a time for mere catch arguments, that time surely is not now. In times like the present one should utter nothing for which he would not willingly be responsible through time and in eternity." In articles titled, "Probing the 'Slap-Tap Flap,' " as well as in the editorial view that "Nixon's luck just ran out," American politics and journalism reek of the catch argument.

A nail can be smashed into such a knot that no carpenter can straighten it. Then it must be taken to a factory, melted down, and recast. Usually the recasting that brings everyone back to his senses and to some concern for the last word is a war, a great war *which someone caused.*

Franz Kafka put the point to our journalists and politicians in *America*: "You must put things more simply, more clearly; the Captain can't do justice to what you're telling him. . . .Take your grievances in order, tell the most important ones first and the lesser ones afterward; perhaps you won't even have to mention most of them." I am taking my grievances in order. I am putting the most important first, and am not mentioning most of them.

Certain governmental agencies consciously deceived us on the four crucial issues just discussed. They deceived us also about their dealings with Sihanouk and Lon Nol, and in Chile, about the planning of coups in Southeast Asia, about the organization of armies to defend regimes with unreported sums of money against indigenous attacks, attacks about which Americans came to live in a world of fantasy. While "secret" bombings were going on in Southeast Asia, Senator Symington showed that, save for the prostration of journalism in this country, the truth could have been brought forward, *even about this:*

First. Most of the war in Laos is coordinated through and by the American embassy in Vientiane.

Second. The United States trains, arms and feeds the Lao Army and Air Force.

Third. The United States, through the Central Intelligence Agency, trains, advises, pays, supports and coordinates an irregular army, elements of which are deployed in four of the five military regions of Laos.

Fourth. The United States, through the Central Intelligence Agency, and in co-operation with the Thai government, trains, pays, supports, and coordinates a growing force of Thai soldiers in Laos.

Fifth. In addition to interdiction operations over the Ho Chi Minh Trail, the U.S. Air Force flies hundreds of combat missions throughout Laos in close support of Lao regular and irregular ground forces. . . —*Congressional Record,* p. S. 15764.

Senator Symington stated that even he could not give figures on our aid to military governments of Southeast Asia, for these figures are kept top secret. A few years later this would be a scandal. Why? A general would sit in the United States Senate and state that yes, he had bombed illegally, and would do so again under similar circumstances. An intelligence-gathering agency conducting war? A general defying senators? How did this come about?

James J. Kilpatrick sees waging of war a proper intelligence-gathering function. After Allende's death in Chile, he wants those "skeletons put back in the closet." Otherwise, some prattling Senator will give away a vital secret.

Of what source of pride are checks and balances, free press, freedom of speech and the rest, if a country travels the road of nationalism, aggressive instincts, militarism, misoneism, and war profiteering anyway? Our country was established, incidentally, by guerrilla warfare. The revolutionaries fired at redcoats from behind hedges and through groves and drove them from the field by ambush and the threat of ambush. Our heroes had not one-tenth the cause to fight against foreign arrogance and economic manipulation of their government which Southeast Asians have had. It was not taxation without representation which angered Vietnamese, it was absentee landlordism without representation. If the Vietnamese were communists, rather than fighters for the democratic ideal, we have no one to blame for that but the West. Communism was a reaction in Southeast Asia.

Is our government truthful? There was, by requisite of logic had to be, at least a tacit agreement that those branches of the military and CIA stationed in Southeast Asia could squander money and interfere in governments of Vietnam, Laos, and Cambodia in ways which allowed Washington to disclaim knowledge and therefore responsibility. Even the President would not have known what was happening there. That is deniability! How clear all this deception was to those who remember things like the *Notstandsgesetze,* the emergency laws which enabled Hitler to sweep away all opposing forces.

Where would Mr. Kilpatrick limit the CIA? *Anywhere?* Does he believe that evil men naturally arise in Germany, but that we in the United States have none and can therefore relax? I can think of no particular reason why social misfits interested in politics and the black arts plagued Germany and Russia and presently plague South America — but do not attempt to find their way into American politics. They *do* try to find their way in, and what channels are most open to them? I believe it is our *system* of government which stops them, and that we certainly do not have James J. Kilpatrick and his colleagues to thank that it still functions.

In politics the little-more-dirt principle is important. Someone does something unscrupulous. Now others are forced to keep pace, and have an excuse. They do something a little dirtier. Then the exclusion principle takes effect. Certain types begin to exclude themselves voluntarily from the mess, and others are excluded by a little more dirt. Then the muck-rises-to-the-top principle begins to operate. Those most ambitious and least principled go farthest. The three principles augment and encourage each other. The degeneration of government continues until a *system* or a war stops it, or until someone contemplates political murder. He who does not understand this remains a child as far as politics is concerned.

At what point would a concerned and righteous president say that the CIA had gone far enough? When it sends assassins abroad? Or would he allow it to compile a list of Americans to be liquidated in a national emergency? Perhaps Richard Nixon did not contemplate the ultimate political crime, but he had created a situation in which, without our safeguards, someone a little less scrupulous than he soon would have. I feel a bit guilty that it was men two hundred years ago who saw this problem and saved us from ourselves.

On its way downward our government passed the point of lying about major issues long ago. To formulate a foreign policy which serves the cause of humanity and democracy in a world in which corruption prevails requires as much effort and expertise as does the design and reckless bartering of weaponry. One cannot discuss this problem with men so caught up in demagoguery, so morally compromised that they can do nothing but justify military solutions. Were the United States to fashion a different policy the circumstances in the world would not immediately change. In the long run the United States would be more secure, could save a great deal of presently wasted economic power, and would not have to massacre the poor. In the absence of a new policy, generals will squander wealth in preparation for a military solution to the problems of our time, and other forces will join the physical force against us. One can practically feel the level of cynicism rising in the world because no one has command of the moral force needed.

The impetus which united communists and capitalists against the Nazis was not purely physical, nor was it purely moral. Vietnam demonstrated again that the force of right can be very powerful in the world. How quickly South Vietnam and the United States could have defeated the North had they possessed moral force in the people's minds! In Vietnam, the United States found, as fascists found, that to have only physical force at one's disposal is a dangerous position to be in.

Public opinion has been a created commodity. It was not a guiding force in the determination of policy. Our government could have reversed public opinion on Southeast Asia almost overnight by releasing the proper arguments and information. It *chose* to deceive.

When one speaks of manipulation, two subjects jump to mind: media and education. Before turning to these subjects in detail, I will add some important variables to our formula, for the above discussion has rendered it inadequate. Colleges, where people read books, blew up like pressure cookers put on to boil with no escape valve when it was found what was happening in

Vietnam. But the great majority of Americans continued to mis-interpret the causes of and also denied the bestiality of the war it waged. The bestiality was all on the enemy's part, the major-ity felt. Here in America we have skillfully designed safeguards against such manipulation of opinion. We have a free press and a system of education which purports to make everyone literate. A liar who can overcome these safeguards is more skilled than one — Adolf Hitler is the best example — who operates under conditions of tyranny and limited educational opportunity for the people.

Then, too, a liar who succeeds in passing off misinformation without resorting to force must be greater than one who needs to liquidate thousands of people wishing to expose him. Such a tyrant as Hitler was in this regard a rather poor liar. At the height of his campaign popularity he received only 43.9 per-cent of the vote, and after he was appointed chancellor — which might be regarded as mere luck — he found it necessary to imprison hundreds of thousands of people who refused to believe him. He could have survived without force just as little as without the help of his pure-capitalist friends. His camps were as necessary to his political career as were the assassina-tions of political opponents. That his party found it necessary to burn down the *Reichstag* — now a historical consensus — shows that as a liar he left a great deal to be desired.

Adding, then, the factors F for brute force and EM for resis-tances such as education and free media, the formula now appears:

$$L = \frac{i \times n \times i_2 \times m \times EM}{F}$$

For my money it is the fourth Great Lie which settles the mat-ter: America must be given credit for far and away the greatest lies ever heard. Great lies have collected about the figure of Paul Bunyan, but these lies are not important. Few people are de-ceived by them. I doubt that even in magnitude they greatly ex-ceed the falsehood in statements made by our governmental spokesmen, and their journalistic defendants, about the Viet-nam War. There are some tall tales about Paul Bunyan, but none more whopping than the story of sending men to defend the fictitious freedom of a nationalistic people, approximately eighty percent of whom our president stated would oppose us — an estimate more or less accurate in 1950, 1954, 1956, or 1960.

The factor d for duration might be added to the formula. If falsehood survives over the years its value climbs. The Great Lies' power to deceive has not been seriously impaired. Americans did not withdraw from the war because they understood the lies, but because they were not winning, because the war was too divisive, too costly, too long. If we had succeeded in permanently crushing Vietnam under a military boot, that would have been termed a success. Thus the lies are withstanding the test of time. They can now rise again, in Chile or somewhere else, to divide us another day.

After the triangle, declares Buckminster Fuller, the strongest figure in nature is the pentagon. I believe him. Each side in itself is only a line, pointing nowhere and forming nothing. Together the Five Great Lies give us our pentagon. It encompasses the truth from which one must begin, if America can extract it.

Newsweek, December 24, 1973

PEKING GOES SHOPPING

Henry Kissinger's cordial dealings with Chinese leaders apparently have touched on a surprising subject: Peking has reportedly expressed interest in buying weapons from the United States. China's needs include tanks, armored personnel carriers and transport planes to give its foot-slogging army more mobility. Reacting to the reports, Pentagon experts express skepticism on two main counts. First, any deal with Peking would require a Presidential waiver of laws that currently ban arms sales to Communist countries. Secondly, China has long been reluctant to rely on outside arms suppliers, preferring to manufacture its own weapons, usually from foreign prototypes. But sources close to Kissinger say that, although Peking has not yet begun full-scale negotiations on purchasing American arms, it has already moved beyond the stage of preliminary soundings.

A certain lack of seriousness . . .

An Essential Vietnam-War Bibliography

No lesser degree of expertise is required for
the application of knowledge than was necessary in its acquisition.
- Konrad Lorenz

The three works most historians consider standard are:

Kahin, Goerge McTurnan and Lewis, John W. *The United States in Vietnam.* 1967.

Buttinger, Joseph. *The Dragon Embattled.* 2 vols. 1967.

Steinberg, David Joel. *In Search of Southeast Asia: A Modern History.* 1971.

Two books contain pertinent documents, along with opinions of a wide variety of politicians, academicians, generals and journalists:

Vietnam: History, Documents, and Opinions on a Major World Crisis. Ed. Marvin E. Gettleman. 1965.

The Vietnam Reader: Articles and Documents on American Foreign Policy and the Viet-Nam Crisis. Eds. Marcus G. Raskin and Bernard B. Fall. 1968.

Conclusions of my essay contained in the section, "War" are based on the three standard works and a selection of other books about American involvement in Vietnam. Among those whose bibliographies and thorough treatment of the war are referred to routinely by specialists in Southeast Asian history is D.G.E. Hall's *A History of Southeast Asia* (1964). A condensation of Buttinger's larger work, *Vietnam: A Political History* (1968), runs to over 500 pages. A reading citizen seeking accurate treatment of the war need not labor through thousands of pages. For an excellent shorter presentation Hal Dareff's *The History of Vietnam: A Background Book for Young People* (1966) would do as well. Essential bibliographic entries in any serious treatment of the war are in my opinion the following:

Buttinger, Joseph. *The Smaller Dragon.* 1958.
Cody, John D. *French Imperialism in Indochina.* 1954.
Devillers, Philippe. *Histoire du Viet-Nam de 1940 à 1952.* 1952.
Fall, Bernard B. *The Two Viet-Nams.* 1963.
Fall, Bernard B. *Vietnamese Witness.* 1966.
Fitzgerald, Frances T. *Fire in the Lake: The Vietnamese and the Americans in Vietnam.* 1972.
Hammer, Ellen. *The Struggle for Indochina, 1940-1955.* 1966.
Lancaster, Donald. *The Emancipation of French Indochina.* 1954.
McAlister, John T. *Vietnam: The Origins of Revolution.* 1969.
Marr, David. *Vietnamese Anti-Colonialism, 1855-1925.* 1971.
Osborne, Milton E. *French Presence in Cochinchina and Cambodia: Rule and Response, 1859-1905.* 1969.
Pike, Douglas. *Viet Cong: The Organization and Techniques of the National Liberation Front of South Vietnam.* 1966.
Shaplen, Robert. *The Lost Revolution.* 1955.
Smith, Ralph. *Viet-Nam and the West.* 1971.
Woodside, Alexander B. *Vietnam and the Chinese Model: A Comparative Study of Nguyen and Ch'ing Civil Government in the First Half of the Nineteenth Century.* 1971.

These books provide coverage of all phases of the war. Perhaps it appears odd that I recommend the reading of certain respected historical works to writers on American foreign policy. Yet I do so with good reason. It is regrettable in the extreme, and a sad commentary on American journalism, that editorialists and politicians continue to expound on Southeast Asia obviously without benefit of the books listed herein.

One approach to be taken in recapitulating the important events of the twentieth century is provided by the biographies of Ho Chi Minh. Those published in communist countries are of course unreliable. But these two, the first by a Frenchman, the second by a German, are reliable and heartbreaking:

Lacouture, Jean. *Ho Chi Minh.* 1968.
Neumann-Hoditz, Reinhold. *Portrait of Ho Chi Minh.* 1972.

A subject deserving attention regardless of how one feels about the Cold War is that of civilian casualties and atrocities. How does one come by accurate information? How were atrocities committed and who killed civilians, when and how often, where and why? Three books will be included here, in the order of emphasis with which they are recommended:

Herman, Edward S. *Atrocities in Vietnam: Myths and Realities.* 1970.

Gerassi, John. *North Vietnam: A Documentary.* 1968.

Race, Jeffrey. *War Comes to Long An: Revolutionary Conflict in a Vietnamese Province.* 1971.

These books deal with the subject of casualties in Vietnam whose official numbers run as released March 30, 1973:

Death Toll
in Vietnam

Saigon (AP) — The total Vietnam War casualties as reported by the allied commands:

American — 45,943 killed in action, 300,640 wounded in action.

South Vietnamese — 166,439 killed in action, 453,039 wounded in action.

North Vietnamese and Viet Cong — 937,562 killed.

Civilians — the U.S. Senate Subcommittee on Refugees estimates civilian casualties in South Vietnam at 415,000 killed and 935,000 wounded from 1965 to 1972. Since the cease-fire went into effect Jan. 28, the Saigon command has reported 460 civilians killed and 1,343 wounded.

Disagreements on statistics such as these, with each side using casualties as a means to support its own view of the war, have contributed to the polarization of American society. Even among objective observers one finds widely varying opinions on statistics. But the disagreements are about numbers. One who reads the books in this bibliography will have little doubt about what factors are responsible for the majority of civilian deaths. Since it is unrealistic to expect all citizens to read each of them, it might be advisable to reduce the number still further. Any of the books by Fall, Shaplen, McAlister, and Fitzgerald would, individually, provide a clear and accurate introduction to issues and events of Southeast Asian history. While the war is as complex as any similar historical problem of that magnitude, it is possible, for reasons I have attempted to develop in my essay,

39

to challenge anyone to find a respectable work anywhere which addresses itself to the five issues discussed in section three without supporting its conclusions. If my essay succeeds in gaining a wider readership for the books listed, its purpose will have been served.

Further bibliographies may be found in several of the books I have selected. Buttinger's *Vietnam: A Political History* contains a useful bibliography and includes commentary on the contents, often on the author and approach of each work listed. The bibliographical essay in Steinberg's *In Search of Southeast Asia: A Modern History* is helpful.

It is necessary to indicate what is not included in this bibliography and why. A personal account of some aspect of the war may help in gap-filling, but I have striven to select historical studies which provide perspective on crucial issues. Halberstam's *The Best and the Brightest* concentrates on personalities of and interactions among various functionaries in American government. *Two, Three . . . Many Vietnams,* by Garrett and Barkley contains an assortment of radical opinions. Such books are interesting. They are not essential to an understanding of the war, and there is something unsettling about the production of 800-page best-sellers on issues about which the last word was spoken years ago.

On the subject of war itself three books excel. They have not, in my opinion, received nearly the attention they deserve, though they have received a good deal.

Storr, Anthony. *Human Aggression.* 1968.

Lorenz, Konrad. *On Aggression.* 1966.

Ardrey, Robert. *African Genesis.* 1961.

Miles Copeland's work on international politics, *The Game of Nations* (1969), demolishes many myths. Mr. Copeland, according to his publisher, "at one time employed by the State Department and a man who helped organize the CIA, former diplomat, businessman, Middle East expert," describes with candor his years in the eye of power struggles. He is one of a growing number of men in government whose writings emphasize the consequence of an enlightened public.

An enlightened public must appreciate the domino theory: dominoes must be lined up and set upon end to be pushed over. Otherwise they may be taken by overwhelming force, but they do not fall. The oldest things under the sun, those forces so laboriously analyzed by ancient Greeks, Shakespeare, historians and now animal behavioralists, are lining up countries like dominoes. If an unreasonable ideology characterized by contempt for individual liberty stumbles into the table and knocks them all over, it will mean the educational failure of western democracy, not the success of monolithic communism.

In deference to Jerome Chase's predilection for the number, I restricted my criticisms to five.

1) My main objection: Almost no one has your dedication to finding the truth. With the best of intentions you have encouraged people to take an oversimplified attitude toward the world of politics. The last word on Vietnam, could it be spoken, would not be the last word on the Middle East, which must be thought out as a matter in itself. In a game of chess any piece may be fatal. Forty years ago the fatal figure was appeasement. Today the pieces have been moved several times, by amateurs, and none of the same reasoning applies. The pawn of growing population has queened, because ignored, and announced checkmate to many nations. This is a problem of third-world nations of their own making, and you saw yourself what they chose to do at the World Food Conference — insist that overpopulation is a fiction invented by industrialized nations while blaming colonialism and economic imperialism for all its ill effects.

Dissenters must not believe that other nations and leaders are wiser or better than ours. Most are not a whit better, and many are much worse. Arabs have proven this. The United States supports Palestinian refugees with twenty-four million dollars, while the Arab nations together provide two million. The Arabs cannot spare one day's oil profits for the refugees, but they will wage war on their behalf. They will not solve their social problems, because they are too busy buying weapons from Russia and the United States. If the United States were a model of virtue and philanthropy, we could do very little about the problems of the Middle East. Recall that your beloved Mark Twain saw troubles lying not with Americans, Germans, Russians, or anyone else, but with the damned human race.

2) History loves to pronounce sentence on the wrong people. Those

less disciplined and principled than yourself will take your Five Great Lies, if they become popular, and do unspeakable things with them if they can. You may as well calm down and watch the villains escape rather than clamor for justice. There is no such thing as justice in international affairs. The Vietnam War was only the latest in a long series of stupid performances, and there will be others. "The only thing which occasionally sets a limit to evil in the world is a balance of evil forces," Schiller concluded.

3) The hope of yours to say the last word rests on the erroneous assumption that there is nothing new under the sun. There are three new things under the sun: advancing technology, explosion of information about man and the universe, and overpopulation. Each of these new things leads to other new things: advancing technology to industrialization, pollution, regimentation, and the hydrogen bomb; the explosion of information to specialization and to a malaise caused by uncertainty about man's position in the universe; overpopulation to the exacerbation of all other problems and the resultant antagonisms. Every person your age is in too big a hurry to find the last word on these matters. Again, beware, or the ignorant will make dogma of your ideas.

4) You have not foreseen many events of the past few years, in spite of knowing the last word, supposedly. You did not foresee the President's resignation, nor his pardoning. There may be some surprises in store for you in the bicentennial political campaigns. You were utterly captivated by Lorenz, Ardrey, and Storr, while these writers have been largely discredited by subsequent works, whose position Ashley Montagu sums up in *Man and Aggression*. Could anything be clearer, you have said, than that this glorified animal *Homo sapiens* develops patriotism as the result of instinct rather than cultural learning? No, that is not agreed upon. Beware of the utterers of last words.

5) But you have done a great service. Many of your points are well taken, and together they help us to appreciate fully the opposing camps in America today.

Since the days when Senator Wayne Morse stood practically alone in the Senate, a high percent of my students has thought about Vietnam and United States politics as Jerome did when he first wrote the essay "Peace with Honor." Jerome would write up a draft of that theme, submit it to his father, then to me, then to a professor of history or English or anyone else willing to read and criticize it, finally to incorporate all their opinions, culling the bad and reworking the good, in a painstaking revision.

If all parents placed emphasis on the educational aspect of schooling as did the elder Chase, the job of a teacher would be much easier. Most parents are content if certain social or vocational benefits accrue from the schooling of their children, with the result that a teacher finds it very difficult to motivate youngsters in, say, courses in German and Russian, or even history and geography, where an appreciation for the many faces of tyranny and the price paid to defeat it might be developed. Most of the material lies far outside the experience of Americans in general, not to speak of those raised in the fifties and sixties. How could I then complain if Jerome worked together with his father, a World War II veteran and widely read man, in putting together a complex assignment?

In the hope of improving our understanding of a large segment of the younger generation, I have brought you one articulate young man's attitude toward the Vietnam War, the Cold War, and the domino theory. He now turns with some insight to his interests media and education, after which the teacher will return with a last word.

Part II

OUR HEALTHY DEBATE

4. Media

Through technical devices like the radio and the loud-speaker, eighty million people were deprived of independent thought.

Huxley, quoting Albert Speer on trial

No one should feel a trace of optimism toward the outcome of the non-democratic anti-Saigon victory in Vietnam. A brawler will likely emerge from the in-fighting there, and he will not wither away. Yet we know what America could conceivably offer the world, which makes it doubly upsetting that she has presented only war to Southeast Asia and bolstered tyranny in many other places. In 1962 Warren Weaver showed what might be done with the thirty billion dollars then estimated necessary to put a man on the moon (*Saturday Review*, August 4). With thirty billion dollars we could have provided:

a 10% raise in salary to every teacher in the United States, from kindergarten through universities, in both public and private institutions . . . 10 million dollars each to two hundred of the best smaller colleges . . . financing of seven-year fellowships (freshman through Ph.D.) at $4,000 per person per year for 50,000 new scientists and engineers . . . complete universities, with medical, engineering and agricultural faculties for all fifty-three of the nations which have been added to the United Nations since its original founding . . . three more Rockefeller foundations at $500 million each . . . thus leaving $100 million left over to popularize science.

Twenty or thirty billion dollars so spent might have greatly augmented the deterrent power of our weapons. Instead we spent much more on a battle which rendered communism impossible to stop in Southeast Asia.

It would require 249 years and four months to count twenty billion dollars at the rate of one ten-dollar bill per second, eight hours a day, 365 days a year. Our expenditures in Vietnam dwarfed that amount and deterred no one. Now an American comedian voices the conservative view, "If we'd declared war in Vietnam, this thing would have ended in a year, because the

military would have taken over. We'd have gone all out, and —
bang, bang, bang — it would have been all over."

A healthy, democratic debate could be conducted on how to
use resources in deterring tyranny. There is much room for disagreement on how to spend money and how to avoid its getting
into the wrong hands. But the debate in this country is not
healthy, for half the debaters suffer from some odd strain
of an age-old madness.

Or does Bob Hope have a point? Let us consider this prevalent "go-all-out" theory a moment. The military may have
been able to invade North Vietnam and avoid World War III
and a confrontation with China, which might well have taken
more of our men in a few days than the Vietnamese could in
ten years. Yes, but our military informed us that over 400,000
North Vietnamese soldiers would have faced us in those jungles;
and we know how easy it was to handle the 175,000 insurgents
we once faced with over half a million soldiers in the South.
Perhaps we could have brought those guerrillas to their knees
by levelling their cities and killing two or three times as many
civilians as we actually did kill. Never mind what government
we were defending in so doing. Never mind how it was treating
60,000 political enemies. Never mind that China would have
been very unlikely to stand by and watch such an invasion on
its border, with millions of fanatical communists ready to
enter the conflict on a word's notice.

A comedian considers himself wiser on military matters
than our military, and he is not alone. Bob Hope, William
Buckley, John Wayne, James J. Kilpatrick — of course it is
not fair to single out individuals. John T. Connor, Commerce
Secretary under President Johnson, gives a prevalent opinion
among prominent personages on Watergate:

Impeachment of the President is not the answer. His impressive record — in handling
the Vietnam troop withdrawal, the return of our prisoners, the establishment of new
hopeful relationships with Russia and China, and the needed realignments of our
foreign and domestic responsibilities — leads inevitably to the conclusion that his
continuity in office is well deserved.

Now these men pride themselves on being realists. Posterity,
unless thinking people find themselves in something like our

present situation, will never adequately appreciate what reasonable people have tolerated in the way of irresponsible public statements during the past decade. If the comedians had had their way, we would have won the war at the price of approaching Germany and Russia as planners of genocidal policy, and those for whom we fought would have been worse off than ever, if they lived. Whether to be oppressed by the local tyrant, hungry, or to join a revolutionary group and so end the slings and arrows of outrageous fortune — that would have been the question facing Vietnamese in their dealings with government, as it was when their war began generations ago.

Healthy, democratic debate flourished while the bombers flew, day after day, year after year. Granted that the conversation must and will continue. At the same time one must point out that courageous defense of an opinion is pointless when one finds oneself up against a wall of men who have blinded themselves. An entire school of editorialists and prominent personalities has united some peculiar opinions in what they present as a realistic philosophy. As conservatives they defend the acceleration of military ventures by an intelligence-gathering agency. They who are supposedly against arrogant use of power in a centralized government wish to brake investigation of clandestine operations destructive of due process.

A released POW spoke for the cause, insisting that if only college kids could experience the indignity of life in a communist country, they would be "the most conservative bunch of college kids in the world." I am not speaking for the liberal cause in replying that he should have been thanking a lucky star he was not imprisoned by Saigon, the system for which he fought.

Unfortunately, I must have more examples to illustrate the sickness of the American debate. Of hundreds of equally suitable editorials, then, consider briefly the one of May 18, 1972, below. Not hundreds, but thousands of equally instructive editorials could easily be assembled. One need only open a newspaper of the sixties to find one.

This editorial does not address the crucial issues. What position does it contain on the origins of the war? On the division

Buckley Gets Reaction To His Vietnam Ideas

By WILLIAM BUCKLEY JR.

I wrote ten days back when the North Vietnamese blitzkrieg was juggernauting south that the United States government has a lot to answer for.

For instance, our highly defic- ient intelligence and military estimates which persuaded most Americans t o believe t h a t V i etnamization was working, the the North V i e t n a m ese were finally up a g a i n s t a militarily suffi- cient South Vietnam. I have 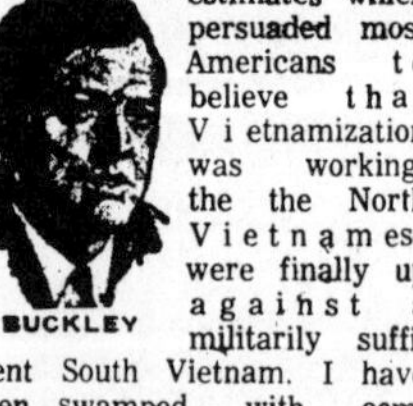 been swamped with com- mentary, the c o m m o n denominator of which is I-told- you-so. The critics bear watching, because it is one thing to · say that our intelligence estimates and the White House reassurances have been delinquent, something else to ar- rive at grand conclusions that would appear retroactively to justify the doves.

FOR INSTANCE there is Miss Gloria Emerson, 'the prominent, talented, and beautiful cor- respondent for the New York Times. She spent two years in South Vietnam deploring every human misadventure, trivial and tragic — except those caused by the North Vietnamese, which I confess struck me all along in a class with deploring corrup- tion among political prisoners at Ravensbruck.

She has cabled me from Lon- don: "I've just read your col- umn asking why we've known so little and why we've mis- judged so gravely in Vietnam. There were in last seven years reporters who at the risk of their own careers let alone their lives tried to tell the truth, not what Washington or Saigon wanted them to say. They were talking to the deaf. You among them and perhaps it would be wise to ask yourself why you for so long preferred to be."

I was not aware that the correspondents in question had risked their careers. Indeed they took quite early to picking up Pulitzer Prizes. But let that go.

ANOTHER correspondent put it more directly, more personal- ly. "What happened in Vietnam, you're asking? That's gall. One thing that happened was that a VIP editor went out there, got his head stuffed full of glow- ing reports, and relayed these back to his constituency in just glowing enough terms to keep alive the tyranny of the majority for just one more round of back- into-the-breach, men."

One sees here a certain righteous and self-serving con- fusion. Those who have been against our engagement in Viet- nam are saying that they also predicted that Vietnamization would not work. Comment: Some did, some didn't. A further and of course necessary observ- ation is that whereas Richard Nixon said Vietnamization was working, while some of his op- ponents said it was not working, the layman had to ask himself: which of the two is likelier to be correct? Gloria Emerson or Richard Nixon?

MISS EMERSON ·(and. others who were categorically against the war) have been tied down very hard to ideological theses. They could·not convincingly con- ceal their desire for the failure of the entire U.S.-South Viet- namese enterprise. If it happen- ed that they guessed wrong, what were the consequences? Hardly shattering. Professor John Kenneth Galbraith flatly predicted in the spring of 1968 after Tet that the government of President Thieu would not sur- vive the fortnight. It has not hurt him, not his prestige or his credibility, that he proved massively wrong.

Richard Nixon, by contrast, stands to lose the presidency, and by correlative default, the United States stands to lose its place as leader of the western coalition, if he is wrong. Who, more likely, would the layman believe? Gloria Emerson or Richard Nixon?

That is one point, the remaining one being something on the order of justice to the South Vietnamese, who are the popular villains these days, not all the correspondents are of the same stripe. For instance there is a former artilleryman in the second world war, a student of security problems, who writes that contempt for the South Vietnamese ill becomes the United States, given our own military experiences. "This reminds me of the Ardennes bulge of 1944-45. Eisenhower then refused to believe what several intelligence agencies had told him, and the result was Bastogne."

STRANGE, that having taken as long as we did to roll back the Nazis, during a period when the French showed rather less determination against the Nazis than the South Vietnamese have shown against the Communists, that we should be so contemptuous of the performance of the ARVN, a n d of our military command.

Even if, when the evidence is in, I judge them to have been critically incompetent, I do not understand how the acknowledgement of this datum delivers me into the arms of Gloria Emerson, however satisfying such a relegation would unquestionably prove.

Defense of a viewpoint is pointless . . .

of Vietnam? Does it investigate why John Kenneth Galbraith incorrectly predicted that the Thieu regime would not survive? Yet in a single editorial Buckley has succeeded in confounding the debate hopelessly. Now the public can never get clear what the captain is saying. No one will be able to present the present *or* historical truth, nor deal with past or present misery in Vietnam, for he will be smugly swatted down. Buckley is not even serious; he ends his editorial with a characteristic sneer in the poorest of taste. Yes, a certain lack of seriousness betrays such men.

On talk shows, Barry Goldwater called Daniel Ellsberg a Benedict Arnold. He gave the impression that we were using only pinpoint bombing in Vietnam. Why are these Buckleys, Waynes, Hopes, Grahams, Colsons, Kilpatricks, Goldwaters and the rest so full of contempt for people who "deplored every human misadventure, trivial and tragic" that happened in Vietnam but not upset about these events themselves? Those who repeat tales like that of the careless grenade-tosser are unrealistic and soft!

Here we have supposed conservatives who want a powerful central government by presidential ukase. If the President can't bribe and infiltrate and wage war through open debate, let him do it through secret agencies organized for different ends than these. He needs an alternative between peace and war!

We read and hear that Watergate has tremendously damaged American government. Not the deception, the misuse of funds, the planned character assassinations and blacklisting of political opponents — no, the *revelation* of these abuses had damaged our government and proved itself a "trauma," according to the conservative columnist. No wonder the public cannot make sense of the news. No wonder we now have a group of Amercans so confident of its position that it considers the search for truth superfluous and speaks arrogantly about the things it misunderstands. It reacts to a deep look into its government's character with: "That sort of thing goes on in business and industry every day." "Some people are bribed by a cup of coffee. Where do you draw the line?" "Roosevelt had a couple of babes on the side. Morally, Watergate is no worse." In response to Saigon treatment of political prisoners and other atrocities: "Now let's have an in-depth study of the terror bombings of marketplaces by the Viet Cong." Or, admitting the seriousness of Watergate: "How could this happen? This bothers me very much. I'm a flag-waver." Finally, my favorite, in response to any accurate analysis: "Well, it's just one man's opinion. Who is he to criticize our experts? It's like a patient advising his doctor how to perform an appendectomy." Yet slowly the President's popularity falls: "His luck has run out." And the war becomes unpopular: "That war is not worth the life of one American aviator." "We burn fuel over Southeast Asia which could heat our Midwest for years." "This man was torn between loyalty to his country and concern for his son."

You cannot have a healthy debate when half the debaters are too misinformed to understand their own words and are so misoneistic that they will not listen when you speak.

A realist is not one who believes the greatest lies one might tell about the origin of a war. He can know nothing if he does not know what he is fighting *for*, if he ignores written agreements and fails to comprehend what the enemy believes is at stake. No realist fails to distinguish between an intelligence-gathering agency and a *geheime Staatspolizei*, a secret state police, which bribes, assassinates, and subverts. An intelligence-gathering agency gathers intelligence.

Someone must apparently write "A Primer on the Human Condition" for syndicated columnists. Of all people, those who termed themselves realists knew the least about reality in Vietnam. Huxley or Orwell or Twain or Rogers would have seen it. They would have looked through Nixon's White House in no time, *without* Watergate. These men were realists. No one who writes month after month, year after year, about such issues, going counter to all historical studies, finally to be proven wrong about most everything, has a claim to the title realist. To debate with him may be necessary on occasion, but to debate with him continually is to degrade yourself and the debate, too.

There would be a complete spectrum of opinion in this country without these men, these "realists." Perhaps because they themselves have lost the capacity to be appalled at injustice and suffering, they expect that all others are *also* feigning their concern, and can be spoofed, parodied, laughed at. Perhaps they are convinced that because they themselves have the sensitivity of a burlap bag, that must apply to all others also. Even if I were to agree with their writing about the war, which would be difficult because they do not discuss the vital issues, I could not escape feeling responsible for the past and present plight of Vietnamese, Cambodians, and Laotians. These men never get around to considering what happened in that part of the world; they are too busy turning others' arguments against them. In their opinion that one must "go all out" and "turn it over to the military," one detects a black hole where concern for the real effects of that policy should be.

Without these men there could have been no Watergate, for the public would have been informed. Our priorities would be different, so instead of appropriating money to arm dictators, some could be saved to present a real deterrent. America would have not entered Vietnam, but would have used sanctions to prevent the dominoes from lining up. America would not be a divided nation today.

All that and more is at stake in a journalistic debate. America could conceivably be a shining light to the world, with the power of a giant and the social problems of a Norway. Instead, her politicians begin their careers as demagogues and end by doing what is in their power to destroy checks and balances. In a healthy debate, all could speak honestly and openly about the complexity of the world's problems. They would not need to lie.

The men discussed here have one thing in common: they are all wealthy, comfortable, educated men, most raised in comfort and used to comfort. This brings my formula to mind. The American people are still economically strong. True, inflation has made some editorialists a bit edgy: "You can almost cut the fear, it's so thick"; "Inflation has chewed the middle class to pieces." They did not understand these things happening elsewhere, but they certainly understand them when they occur here in the United States! Several historical parallels could be cited to show that *now* one might begin to watch for liars. The Germans turned to them in desperation. Be that as it may, we need to add another factor to our formula for measuring lies: prosperity. Demagogues have had a notoriously difficult time leading people astray during times of prosperity. They have usually had to wait for a wealthy class to destroy the economic basis for the majority's existence, whereupon everyone becomes angry enough to listen to lies. But this has not been the case here. Far from it. Our liars were so effective they didn't require a time of economic and political chaos. They operated on the principle that if most were sufficiently satisfied they would believe anything, and the rest could do nothing.

The several journalists and comedians listed are all quite wealthy men. They have the leisure to pursue the truth, yet they invariably come up with a catch argument, some half-truth which others must attempt to rebut. Our formula for measuring lies must therefore include the factor *p* for prosperity:

$$L = \frac{i \times n \times i_2 \times m \times EM}{F} + p$$

The American media have problems other than the closed-mindedness of half the debaters. One need not analyze the reversal of the overheated image to understand the media's difficulty with the catch argument and the half-truth. My favorite quotes show how tempting and dangerous they are.

Hegel developed the idea that truth exists in the totality. Editorialists, however, deal with bits and scraps of news as they appear. In a book one can discuss lies individually and in combination, then *in toto*. Because a writer cannot scratch the surface of ethnocentrism through his best efforts, cannot upstage the media and overcome selective reading, William James wrote:

Every up-to-date dictionary should say that "peace" and "war" mean the same thing, now *in posse*, now *in actu*. It may even reasonably be said that the intensively sharp competitive *preparation* for war by the nations *is the real war*, permanent, unceasing; and that the battles are only a sort of public verification of the mastery gained during the "peace"-interval.

Yet he added, "I myself think it our bounden duty to believe in . . . international rationality as possible."

A controlled press derives its insidious effects on public opinion by presenting the only available version of everything — *the* official version. Trapped people, denied basic freedoms of speech, assembly, and the press, create fatalistic sayings. A substantial number of Germans responded to "Germany, Germany above all," with "Two potatoes is about all." "If it's in *Pravda*, it can't be true," circulates through Moscow, a safe attitude to take when everyone with action-taking power, everyone allowed to speak, is propagandizing. The word "Pravda" means "truth."

Another important Soviet newspaper is *Izvestia*, a word meaning "news." Thus the Russian quip: "In the *News* there is no truth, and in the *Truth* no news." Here is food for thought.

What if Russians were not commenting on Soviet media, but on news reporting in general? If you seek the causes of things, you will find no news. If you read fabricated news, or even accurate news of our battle with communism, you will find — well, what will you find? Shall we seek the causes of events by searching for them, or by establishing the grain of truth in our view of today's events, as our leading news magazines do? "There is a grain of truth in all these theories," says *Time* magazine in its analysis of the Cambodian insurrection. One could as easily become an oceanographer by sitting on the sand watching waves.

A thousand catch arguments and half truths have in the American media added up to the five big lies concerning Vietnam and the Cold War. Media should possibly be discussed in a digression termed "the catch argument" under the rubric "truth in government." How can one counter pro-war arguments constantly appearing in the media today? In a letter-to-the-editor? In an editorial? How can one show that we were not fighting another Nazi Germany in Vietnam? If a war hawk can be induced to listen to an exposition of one point, he will remain as before because that point will be like one side of a geometrical figure: standing by itself, what can it say? Regarding the lies as one Great Lie, in Hegel's sense, means considering lies one, two, and three — those regarding the nature of the war and the nature of what we fought for in the South — surprisingly straightforward, matters which can be discussed in writing though hardly at all in heated argument. The first three lies are of historical interest, except that their long-run hegemony over American thought leads one to fear that they will be replaced by other, equally obvious and harmful lies. Lies four and five, on misconceptions of modern warfare and the functioning of our own government, are of more than historical interest. They bring in moral questions and help explain why Americans would accept fallacious interpretations of *any* war or *any* foreign policy, as long as it was endorsed by the White House.

We cannot fault our best and wisest journalists for not making issues clearer, but we can recognize *with them* that one does not get at the truth by watching television and reading newspapers alone. We also cannot learn much from the vast communications media in Hollywood concerned with manipulating the public's emotions for the sake of box offices and ratings.

Hollywood creates one grim-eyed hero after another for young and old to identify with. Enlightening discussions must ensue from consideration of the totality of the five lies. Together the five points take on momentum — a moving pro-war freight train of momentum if the falsehood is uncritically accepted and combined with love of country and hatred of The Enemy; an oppositely traveling train if all the lies are rejected and seen as countless small lies carrying a great payload of intellectual dishonesty. Herein we ascertain the ingredients of a domestic collision, in spite of a free press. We can understand from consideration of disagreements on the totality the bitterness of polarization and why it will linger on long after the signing of a peace treaty. It is understandable why certain people who opposed the war all along bristle at protestations of Nixon's "fine performance" in bringing about a peace settlement, and why they throw up their hands at the frequently heard assurance that a supporter of the war, Gerald Ford, after pardoning his predecessor, will "clean up" the mistakes made.

Gerald Ford's conciliatory speeches contain many barbs aimed at those who have disagreed with him for the last fifteen years. Meanwhile programs like "The F.B.I." guide the public into a good-versus-evil view of the world which has *never* been accurate. "You look at what I'm looking at, but you do not see what I see," says the hawk. And the dove responds in kind.

President Eisenhower warned about the military-industrial complex, but he should have warned again and again on the grounds that no one was listening. Enough secondary issues related to this question have been introduced to provide a carnival for ethical relativists and journalists more interested in filling newspapers than in discovering and propounding the truth. Were not men like William Crum and the police-chief executioner exceptions to generally well-intended — if misguided — maneuverings of our diligent military and the competent Saigon government in assigning duties? How do we know for sure the causes and truth of My Lai? The soldiers were under terrible stress. That fact stands. Did similar incidents of lesser gravity really occur as frequently as the Veterans Against the War would have us believe? Were the people of the South really so dead-set against having Americans in their country, did they *really* hate military men in Saigon so much that Vietnamization was doomed to failure? Have not the North Vietnamese also committed atrocities? Was Vietnamization a fiction created to sway public opinion in America? Has government in the North not been corrupt also? What percentage of anti-Saigon forces were soldiers recruited from the populace of the South? Did men fight more willingly for the North or the South? How did Eisenhower know for sure about Ho Chi Minh's popularity? How do we know for sure that he was a national hero? Were leaders in Washington and the military in Saigon blamelessly trapped by events beyond their control? Was President Johnson a tragic figure with an excellent domestic record?

One more question: Could journalists and news commentators find in these and dozens of other questions food for argument, for quibbling between liberals and avowed conservatives, to fill the newspapers for a hundred years and still come to no conclusions about one of the most clear-cut of wars? Perhaps

this has become what the animal behavioralists say it is — basically an expensive kind of entertainment illustrating, in Mark
Twain's words, man's descent from the higher animals. Even
singly, and certainly in their totality, the Five Great Lies will
stand in history approximately as described in Part I of this
book. They are the issues of the war, quibble with my wording
as you will. If something conclusive can be said about them
one has an argument with force. George C. Marshall had seen
the last word, whether the questions themselves were to be con-
fused in two more decades of sickening debate or not. Marshall's successors were too much the politicians to wrest control
from a military-industrial complex, as President Eisenhower
advised, and return it where it belonged — with an accurately
informed citizenry. Marshall knew that if one stomps upon an
already crushed people, twenty years later madness will arise
as in a Japanese horror movie, and the world will pay again.
In the Five Great Lies one can perceive the causes of the war,
as Eisenhower already had, none of which could be affected
by an answer to questions on the Gulf of Tonkin incident,
nor in angry discussions of atrocities, nor in condemnation of
intransigence in North Vietnamese negotiators. Enough information has been available on the five main issues to make
possible a judgment as certain as any historical judgment can
ever be, relativists notwithstanding. One can ask oneself all
the above and countless other quibbling questions about the
particulars, laying pebbles on the rails to derail a freight-train
argument. The lies will remain Great Lies. No politician who
chooses to confound vital issues with secondary ones will bring
us all together, restore confidence, or even convince us that res-
toring confidence in government is the main task at hand,
because too many people — those who view lies as lies and call
each child by his right name — now hate public lying. If you discard the truth about crucial issues, all else follows, all the way
to My Lai.

Where does a small nation turn when America places her
full weight behind the many forms of tyranny? A perceptive
person, having understood the question, does not seek to excuse
governmental dishonesty in America, atrocities, and war itself
by bickering about epiphenomena. The objection that he has

no right to know, that the government must decide without public knowledge, secretly, is the last insult to his intelligence. He looks for ultimate causes and eats his helping of despair when the atrocities finally occur which he *knew* had to accompany a war caused by misinformation on central issues. He expects humanity from neither side, atrocities from uneducated, heavily armed, teen-aged men of whatever nation when these are trapped in a desperate cultural collision. Writers using the enemy's atrocities to quibble about the particulars of Song My, bickering about the frequency of atrocities, seeking to point out the exceptional nature of Ky's statement about Hitler, in order to excuse the tyranny of Saigon and confound the written agreements on the division of Vietnam — these adopt at best intellectually dishonest approaches to finding the truth, evil at worst, and can in no case establish a total, historically based view of the war.

Without an increased public awareness of our government's habit of answering each threat in the world by spending billions for military aid, espionage, and clandestine operations to support vested interest and the status quo, while allowing big oil and big aviation companies to spend millions on politicians here and abroad, future administrations can continue to replace troops with an intensification of diplomatic and technological warfare, all for the benefit of special interests in the United States. The results will be more leaders turning to the communists for aid, as Sihanouk has done, because the United States is the great power involved when coups oust their leaders and replace them with generals of the character of Lon Nol, a man who recently took his newly acquired wealth and emigrated. *These* are the issues which must be dealt with in any healthy debate, because they are *the* issues of the Cold War period. They leave room for a broad spectrum of views without the Buckleys, Goldwaters, Waynes, Fords, Wallaces, and Reagans. I can see why some journalists are peeved at lack of confidence in their statements, and why they are more angry at people saying "I told you so" than at the compilers of the White House enemies list.

If these super-patriots had been born in Germany or Russia, who could they have been? Two hundred years ago they would almost certainly have been loyal to the British crown; that was the conservative cause in those days. For the aware citizen, the Gulf of Tonkin Resolution was more serious than Watergate. The presidential pardon of General Lavelle after his illegal bombings was another Watergate — or worse, for it cost taxpapers much money and many human beings life and limb. Our pay-offs to Lon Nol were more serious than Watergate, for they brought war to another country. One should need no scandal to tell one that. The way body counts were compiled, the insistence of the Pentagon that Susiimi, highest French official in North Vietnam, was killed by a falling SAM missile — this list of major and minor Watergates could be extended to any length. Indeed, cover-up of CIA activities in Saigon, Phnom Penh, and Vientiane is of such sweeping nature that it might be considered a sixth Great Lie.

If I had written that Christmas bombings of civilian populations were a proper response to communist "Mickey Mouse" at the root of difficulties in Asia, I, too, would be embarrassed at a truthful look into our government's heart. If my position could be sunk by a quirk of fate (the capture of a few government burglars) I, too, would be defensive and therefore a bit offensive. Mr. Buckley, Mr. Kilpatrick, and others of the same persuasion have been to journalism what Nixon's plumbers were to American politics. For years the United States could not negotiate with its enemies, whose thinking revolved about the issues of outside interference, oppressive conditions in the South, unity. One can debate forever, through 60 Minutes or for twenty years, whether ex-Colonel Herbert or the Pentagon is lying, but that only sets everyone up for a jolt when the freight train of truth arrives to find us laying pebbles on the rails: as far as winning the hearts and minds of people, the United States military has been the communist conspiracy's most persuasive advocate.

The *news* is that Kissinger flies to Paris. The *truth* is that disagreements on the division of the country have fouled peace talks for years, and so fouled the peace settlement that it looks like continued war. Kissinger skirts the issue by saying that only certain "disagreements on the DMZ" are blocking progress. The Viet Cong, however, by the basic logic of their position, will remain adamant in wanting connections between Saigon and America severed.

The *news* is that Nixon meets with Thieu. What they say no one knows. Each will make his carefully worded public announcements. The American public and press will carefully consider these statements. The *truth* is that we have supported a series of opportunists in Vietman, and that Thieu, too, will do his best to concentrate power in his own hands by closing critical presses, rounding up suspected sympathizers for his camps, and imprisoning critical legislators, finally to take his millions and look into a home in Hawaii.

To find the truth one must look back to '63, then back to '54, '46, and before. What have the main issues been for Vietnamese *since Versailles*? Of course, all this is "nothing new" and may receive no attention for that reason. And it is hindsight, though equally available to leaders who escalated the war in the '60s, who had just as much perspective on '45, '46, '54, and '56 as we do now plus one advantage: what had happened in those years was fresher in everyone's memory, and there was still time to do something about the situation.

When you hear someone say, "We should have gone in to win," think of American media. When at the barber shop men curse "the damned communists on campus" who have caused so much trouble, think of media. Media provide four reasons for such reactions to today's current events: first, there has been little truth in the news, which by nature does not yield the causes of events. Second, our healthy debate has been confounded by a group of realists who have blinded themselves. Third, good journalists are restricted to catch arguments and half-truths by the format they are given, and because they must respond not to the challenge of presenting truth, but to the catch arguments of politicians and other journalists. Finally, the truth is not entertaining like the news.

It is unsettling, not entertaining, to find that the *real* F.B.I. decided to infiltrate college students and leave the mafia alone. We all know detective work is dangerous and difficult. But imagine: "Your impossible mission, Jim, should you choose to accept it, is to throw rocks and wave pistols about in college demonstrations, so that the public will regard these [expletive deleted] kids as the bums they are." I think it is time to forget the television F.B.I. for a while, and get the real F.B.I. back in line.

A brief summary of the five crucial issues described by our pentagon, amounting to a synopsis of historical studies, could have been used by the media to create quite a different public attitude toward current events. Conceivably. But Americans wanted to believe their leader. They accepted falsehood in a time of prosperity, with an academic elite expounding its views, under a democratic electoral process and supposedly in a society espousing some form of the Judeo-Christian ethic, in spite of a free press and education for all.

The truth would not have solved Vietnam's problems in the sixties. Insight into the pentagon might have made it possible to address honestly and perhaps eventually attack the problems. Because the pentagon does not yield up its secrets readily, there can be only one long-term hope for democracy.

5. Education

One day better men will call on better men to rule them.
Johann Pestalozzi

At Haiphong on November 23, 1946, French troops heralded the Indochina War by firing at random into and about the city, killing no fewer than 6,000 civilians. The figure is inexact, for reasons Buttinger explains:

The French threw everything they had into the battle for Haiphong — infantry, tanks, artillery, airplanes, and even naval guns, which fired at Vietnamese sectors where there was no fighting at all. Even civilians who had managed to reach open terrain outside the town were fired upon by the naval guns because they were mistaken for soliders missing for an attack. The controversy about the number of Vietnamese

The French mistook fleeing civilians for soldiers massing for an attack. Now it appears to me that the grain of truth in their mistake might well serve as the last word on the war.

The truth, labyrinthine or simple, has been easily available in the many studies of the subject. No one has classified, burned or impounded them; no *Reich's Ministry for Education and Public Instruction* has rewritten them to conform with a party line. The drift of my discussion of media may therefore have been somewhat misleading. The information was there; the truth everywhere to be seen. It follows that I should put down my gratitude to *Time, Inc.* and *Newsweek Magazine* for allowing me to draw from their pages. If our government corrects its errors, this correction will be due to the courage of a small number of men and women, among them journalists of the *Washington Post*. They saw an opportunity, and they *did* something. My hat is off to them. I feel sure they will forgive me for "Media."

Always enough information was there, if people had been minded to evaluate it. If the media represent the promise of the present, education, as ever, remains the promise of the future. No country was ever in a better historical or economic position to offer education for all than America. No country ever planned to do so much with that opportunity educationally. Therefrom proceeds the deduction that no country has more ignominiously failed at that task than America. Thus the ugliness from which people fled to America took firm root here. Educational reform is nonetheless the most basic kind of reform, for "Public opinion is everything. With public sentiment nothing can fail; without it, nothing can succeed" (Lincoln); and "Against stupidity even gods battle in vain" (Schiller). If an ignorant public, then survival of the most corrupt in politics. Lincoln's attitude toward the relationship between politics and education can be summed up briefly: If ignorance prevails, then manipulators, the greedy, and the unscrupulously avaricious and ambitious will simply push honesty off the market. That is the nature of the beast politics. If there exists an ignorantly patriotic public, then scum rises to the top, exceptions like Lincoln demonstrating the law.

Unfortunately, Lincoln, too, saw himself forced to proceed from the negative. It was not his fault. Progress always begins with a negative statement. Before God saw the light and said, "It is good," he must have surmised, "Darkness is bad." Founding fathers were intellectuals who saw the same principles with Lincoln and God and attempted to base a plan for representative government on them. The first step in defense of human dignity was, of course, to rid America of overbearing outsiders meddling in her affairs, draining struggling colonies for Britain's benefit. Immediately thereafter the founding fathers ranked establishment of representative government — a system based on checks and balances dreamed up by Montesquieu — depending for its survival and integrity on an enlightened populace. Freeing ourselves from the redcoats came first, a negative task Americans forgot when dealing with smaller countries.

Americans are not genetically distinct from other peoples. We *are* other peoples. If we are wiser or better, that cannot be due to birth, but to something *learned*. A study of New Europe by David Harman at Harvard demonstrated that about half the adults there are now illiterate — that is, cannot read such eleventh-grade-level materials as one finds in "driving manuals, newspapers and job applications." The study was endorsed by the United States Office of Education, whose former director, James E. Allen, Jr., condemned elementary schools across the country for failing to observe children's "right to read."

Now the estimate "fifty percent illiterate" appears outlandishly high. Whether the exact number of people who cannot read at the eleventh-grade level is five percent or fifty percent does not matter as much as certain other things. It matters precious little whether a citizen *can* read or *cannot* if in fact he does *not* read. And something in human nature causes people to *want* to believe the best about their leaders and the worst about their enemies. Something impairs the judgment of the hawkish journalist — perhaps ethnocentrism, perhaps concern for the reputation of what he has written these twenty years.

Americans certainly do not want to see their country become a New Europe; but one encounters the universal underlying forces in human behavior everywhere, and that includes here. For thousands of years philosophers and historians have written about them. Shakespeare and the ancient Greeks told about Watergates. History is one long series of them. Every generation forgets — that is, it starts from scratch as happy children who have not heard the bad news and would not understand it if they did. Children must come to view historical events from evolutionary, historical, psychological, philosophical, and other perspectives. The knowledge is at hand; the asymptotic curve toward the last word has been plotted.

Ideas which eventually become systematized and receive a logical foundation often originate in a bizarre, unsystematic manner. For instance, a chance statement by a stranger, not even directed at me, once not only dampened my enthusiasm for billiards, but began an unpleasant train of thought eventually culminating in my reappraisal of the classical educational ideal. Already aggravated by my losses at snooker, I heard the stranger say, "In this pool hall everyone is trying to prove he's good."

Philosophy in a pool hall? The more I thought about the arrogant statement, whose reflective tone so ill befitted the locale, the more I regretted its apparent truth. How could an off-the-cuff remark be so simple, so direct, so startling and so true? An expert pool player is indeed, I reflected, usually a hustler attempting to deceive anyone and everyone, or a spoiled child, quite likely both. He humiliates you systematically and as slowly as possible, and cheerfully relieves you of your cash. Loss among pool players is taken with about the maturity of the world's nationalistic soccer fans.

Soon the wisdom in the stranger's comment had ruined the game for me. It too accurately depicted the pool world I had seen. I again play snooker, with more enjoyment than before, for I don't get taken — at least not so often. But the stranger's proposition still accurately depicts for me the world of politics. It too accurately depicts a world based philosophically on an old European educational ideal.

The *Gymnasium* of Germany and the *lycée* of France treat splendidly the foundation stones of western civilization and create highly perceptive minds. Their products are deservedly esteemed for their scholarly output. But nowhere is a hierarchy of educational problems based on man's basic motivating forces less likely to be appreciated than in Europe, where rebels find only Marx as a guide, where social scientists disregard the effects of overcrowding, and where professors claim pompously that "natural science tells me nothing." In the words of Hermann Kant, much of European education is a loud "pfui to the mundane."

Let me repeat: If western democracy fails that failure will be an educational one.

Later encounters with the major philosophers of western civilization have often reminded me of my experiences with billiard players; billiard players have in turn been central to my understanding of philosophers. I slowly heard the bad news and assimilated it, as my father did under fire in the Battle of the Bulge. How many works of art, how many philosophies have found their origins in random thoughts, uttered in such odd surroundings as, say, a pool hall? A systematic thinker might construct a great edifice on the subject of competition, the Peter principle, and political machination, ordering conspicious consumption, the exclusion principle, and the little-more-dirt principle into a framework supported, perhaps, by "the will to power" or "conspicuous consumption" as central concepts — all because he knew from his own experience what it means to be a poor loser. To one insight into human behavior more and more can be added. The only requisites are unusual powers of observation, a propensity for logical thinking, and the ability to use words like "catharsis" and "sublimation."

The problem of competition bothers many people who do not understand human motivation any better than scholars who ignore the pool-hall origins of literature and philosophy. The dilemma arising from the difficulty in determining an ethically good action, in a pool hall or in a bitterly competitive society generally, disturbs every perceptive person: is it a chess tournament, a college chemistry class, or spelling contest? It could pain one that in competition the mere egotistical desire to win overrides enjoyment of the task, concern for the benefits and feelings of others, even consideration of the final effects of the competition on one's own life and personality.

It could pain one that competition extends into idealistic endeavors such as writing essays, into scholarly publication, and into political elections. Do not most authors admit that they write primarily for the satisfaction of recognition? Is it not in the last analysis downright primitive how the citizens of Kansas City and I react when the Chiefs meet the Raiders — this desire of spectators to be on the winning side? And is it not a shame that Joe Namath and Richard Nixon exult equally in the statement, "We're number one!" no matter what being number one entails?

Let me not carry this too far. At worst, bruised dignity results from competition on the pool table. Non-critical injuries ensue from competition on the gridiron. We can tolerate that. Let men risk their lives on mountainsides and striving for the moon. They know the risks. They are not little children fleeing from a horror they cannot understand, which happens when the intra-specific dominance struggle in man carries over into the realms of international politics, inter-racial conflicts, academic scholarship, and the field of education. Let men and women engage in conflict of every imaginable kind. In these last-named fields, however, let them think of a few things besides emerging victorious.

Again borrowing from Twain, why is it that so little of the earth is in possession of its rightful owner? Cultural learning falls short as an explanation. How is it that the United States government misled the public on all the most decisive points while granting irrelevant detail, so that citizens could become both certain and wrong, convinced of falsehood and patriotic? Possibly because the human race is still ignorant of the important things. These important things can be found in serious study of most any subject, if one sticks with it. Study of the German language alone soon leads to the study of German history, which includes the Holy Roman Empire and much else. History to literature, which discusses everything at length. One must take this task seriously, not rank it somewhere below athletics and the senior prom.

Why cannot schools deal with the important subjects? Graduated instruction, one of Europe's finest developments, might be introduced through a little selective cultural borrowing, for one thing. Lorenz *et al* recommend that everyone's education include the development of complete understanding of some basic forces in behavior, forces which they say apply to artisans, FBI agents, protesters, and presidents. To achieve such a goal one would have to overcome a fragmented curriculum which reduces world history to a superficial year of classes, and which allows about one in fifteen of the students who begin a foreign language to complete four years. In the German *Volksschule*, justly lambasted in comparative-education studies as little more than vocational training, two thirds of the pupils take four or five years of English. The American secondary school is unmatched throughout the world for its flippant attitude toward such subjects as history and foreign language. Its products enter society believing that they have twelve years of *schooling* behind them!

No wonder they swallow as adults Madison Avenue's hoax that pleasure is the road to happiness! Pagan Greek hedonists would have laughed at the idea. They knew that happiness comes from the feeling of a job well done, and that those who pursue pleasure end in the misery of self-reproach as often as not. Most of today's college students cannot write, don't know they cannot or don't care. If a class is not entertaining they consider dropping it for something more immediately gratifying. Unless he builds up some skill through his years of education, a pleasure-seeking student will end in misery one way or another.

On the other hand, students often complain that there is nothing they can say or do to move supporters of the most truculent foreign policy, often including their own parents. I have written this treatise to meet that need. If someone says, "We should have gone in to win" — give him this book. If he does not throw it away before page twenty, perhaps he will reconsider his views in the light of old evidence. He lives in a democracy which depends on his perspicacity.

Which brings back the formula. It is one thing for a *desperate* people to overthrow a government, only to see it fall into the hands of the most ruthless, as happened to the Russians. It is one thing for a *desperate* people to be manipulated or frightened by street-fighting, so that a tyrant arises who promises law and order and leads them to disaster. Such people are only partly responsible for the unpredictable, uncontrollable actions of a few. But for a people to take a healthy democracy and make of it a factory for weaponry to be unleashed on a country of peasants seeking independence and lacking even the rudiments of an air force — well, that is the moral equivalent of genocide. One might measure the moral equivalent of genocide M_e in a democracy D by measuring the success of liars L in that democracy, as follows:

$$M_e \cong L = \left(\frac{i \times n \times i_2 \times m \times EM}{F} + p \right)^D$$

The idea of incorporating r for religion must, in my opinion, be rejected. The Christian religion should ideally offer great resistance to nationalism. Whenever people are faced with a choice between God and country, however, they choose country every time. A factor so predictable would be of no use in the formula. It would not so much an enable us to distinguish between Americans and Europeans. Perhaps that is because religion is culturally acquired, while patriotism carries the power of an animal drive. Perhaps. Sartre would say that at some time Americans made a decision to rely on emotions before intellect.

I must break this off. I had planned to suspend judgment and wait, but this is too much. For one thing, ignorance dissolves any formula for measuring morality. Erich Fromm stopped himself at the same point in *The Sane Society*:

If a highly advertised brand of toothpaste is used by the majority of people because
of some fantastic claims it makes in its propaganda, nobody with any sense would say
that the people have "made a decision" in favor of the toothpaste. All that could be
claimed is that the propaganda was sufficiently effective to coax millions of people
into believing its claim.

Most Americans would not know where Vietnam *is* had our administrations not involved them there. But I do not believe that Germans, Russians, Vietnamese, Chinese, or Japanese have deserved what happened to them in this century either, so let the formula stand, if only as a reminder.

Anti-Jewish sentiment in Germany was surely no more widespread or intense than anti-black sentiment in America. The ordinary German did not lynch Jews; hand-picked agents had to do the dirty work. None of the nationalities just mentioned could know how leaders would execute policies once in power. Neither did Americans. The system of checks and balances formulated during the Enlightenment has survived two centuries of heavy pressure from nationalism, racism, and power politics as bad as we see anywhere, and saved Americans from plunging into a bottomless chasm. They are justly proud that it has lasted two hundred years. On one point Jerome is in my opinion correct: Progress must be based on enlightenment, not on what Hemingway called the foolish notion that because the airplane is faster than the horse, the world is getting better.

Hemingway has not been the only writer to see education as a prerequisite of progress, if that was his view. In a few pages I can only provide a few reflections on why this is so, not solutions to specific educational problems. For the sake of children, I will not hide from the moral implications. An almost endless list of not so amusing anecdotes about moral terpitude leading to carnage, economic collapse, and revolution could be compiled to illustrate the connection between ignorance and political events. Retreating from Moscow, Napoleon passed an earlier battlefield, Borodino, still strewn with the rotting bodies of twenty thousand or more men and many thousands of horses, and remarked, "In three weeks this, too, will be forgotten." Now leading columnists insist that we forget Vietnam. The French people apparently never heard of that country or of Borodino, for less than one in ten of Napoleon's

Grand Army soldiers made it back to France from the Russian campaign, while French journalists were much like Americans — they forgot. If they survived Borodino, General Kutuzov, and the Russian winter, they would find themselves still following Napoleon when he re-entered France. In the twinkling of an eye Napoleon would be leading a new army to Waterloo. If the French remembered Waterloo very long, they finally forgot it thoroughly, for some generations later they were firing howitzers into the civilian sectors of Haiphong — where they had about as much business as Napoleon had in Moscow — and naval guns at the fleeing civilians.

A tragic view of history might save mankind from endless repetitions of these events. Nietzsche was right: when man loses his tragic view of history, he becomes a patriot, a dangerous beast once again. He has two ways to learn — through books and the hard way. So far only the hard way has sufficed. Each lesson is lost to the next generation, the exceptions proving the rule.

Joseph de Maistre, a political analyst in Russia in the early part of the nineteenth century, doubted that czarist leadership and the injustices of serfdom, which czars and the nobility attempted to ignore and conceal from westerners, would have no repercussions. He wrote that Russia could be compared to a dead horse, frozen for the time being. But one day, he declared, the horse would thaw and "fill the entire world with its terrible stench." Long after his death, Joseph de Maistre's forecast came true.

If a future generation dislikes billiards, mountainclimbing, and space travel, it can turn to history for entertainment. It need not create new catastrophes. We have many learned men who considered the Vietnam War to be inevitable. Embittered revolutionaries may draw the same conclusion and destroy governments, but they will not improve things much in the long run without some type of new enlightenment.

Napoleon gave France a great body of civil law. There is a great deal of truth in the opinion that this was his only achievement of note. He certainly bolstered Russia's support of her czars. He also attacked a moribund order in the Germanies, and helped keep it moribund.

Peter the Great killed his own son because the boy was a milquetoast, too much a sissy to rule a nation. Frederick the Great's father nearly did the same; and a story of Ivan the Terrible reveals the nature of many Russian czars. A messenger came to report the course of a war. Supposedly Ivan wanted to know what was transpiring, but he was similar to American presidents in one regard: he did not like to hear bad news. The great czar grasped a long, heavy spear standing by the doorway and drove it through the messenger's unsuspecting foot, nailing him to the floor. Then he forced the impaled man to finish reading the bad news before withdrawing the spear. This story may be apocryphal, but it is also the mildest tale on record of Ivan's predilection for torturing people. The CIA's junta friends in South America could have learned from him.

In an enlightened public, past catastrophes would suffice. New ones would not be necessary.

The father of Frederick the Great did not know this. He could not stomach his son's softness. He tried by every means at his disposal to change bookish young Frederick, forcing him to hunt wild boar in freezing rain, throwing his son's French books into the fireplace, and beating anyone who failed to aid him in raising the boy to be a proper ruler. Finally the lad was sufficiently frustrated to arrange with a close friend a headlong flight to France — the home of cultured people, he thought. Both were caught. Now Frederick's father was really angry. He forced his son to look on while the companion was led to the block and decapitated. It worked. Young Frederick pulled himself together, grasped the reins of power, and waged war.

The elder Frederick is famous as the Prussian with the Regiment of Giants. He had a particular fascination for big men in uniform, so he formed a single regiment of them — each man something like six feet, six inches tall or over — which he paraded about proudly. His recruiters came across a giant cabinet-maker one day, but were surprised to discover that this man did not wish to receive preferential treatment from Frederick, King of Prussia. He wanted to build furniture, and if possible, to live a civilized life. Finally the recruiters tricked him into building a trunk and climbing into it as a demonstration of its size, then slammed the lid shut and carried him off in the direction of Berlin. Like so many stories of humor in uniform, this one does not have a happy ending. When they had transported the unwilling soldier far enough that he could be handled safely, they opened the box. He had suffocated. History does not say, but the recruiters probably buried him in the box he had made to their specifications. The Prussian military was like the American in one regard: it was sometimes frugal, and in this case wished to avoid publicity.

One thing we must say for Napoleon, Ivan, Peter, and Frederick: they were realists like Presidents Johnson and Nixon. They only did what they *had* to do, were only riding a popular wave of support which would have washed ashore much flotsam without them. They could not have grasped the core of rationalist philosophy — the self-fulfilling prophecy. Only a dreamer would have brought up the subject in their presence.

By rocketing astronauts to the moon, Americans showed the world what their powerful economy can do when they work together and build upon the total scientific knowledge gathered by nations throughout history. An interesting aspect of this achievement disproves the philosophy which staunch conservatives have sold America — that only vast wealth in private hands can provide adequate incentive for great undertakings.

Consider the way Norway handles the responsibility of her newly found oil. That is the way a civilized nation behaves in the second half of the twentieth century. Oil will not waylay the Norwegian Parliament as lobbyists beat through the doors of representatives with ill-concealed bribes. Norwegians will not put up with it. The boost to the economy will furnish an opportunity for a few to become quite wealthy on a natural resource, but not to the detriment of representation, environment, and national ethics. Norwegians will not be one-sided or closed-minded. They will get the oil together, as Americans went to the moon together.

Certain corporations have been caught. Consider: Over a million dollars given by one company to Honduran officials in order that an export tax be lowered. It will be no news to many, but I would like to explain to my satisfaction what that means. It means that the banana pickers, and those who load the boats, and every checker of fruit, and probably everyone else except government officials must work for next to nothing. The bananas can then be bought by our companies for a pittance and sold in the United States for top dollar. Consider further: Lockheed Aircraft admits to "giving $202 million in commissions, payoffs and bribes to foreign agents ... Admits that $22 million of this sum went for outright bribes." Hogwash. *All* of it went for bribes, and probably more. Lockheed makes jets for the military. Lockheed is paid by the United States taxpayer. That means *your* tax dollar is being used to ensure that governments around the world are run by men who take bribes and buy jets. Why? To protect themselves from banana pickers. Exxon paid $740,000. Northrop, $30 million. McDonnell Douglas, $2.5 million. Gulf Oil, $4 million. Little Ashland Oil, $300,000. (Source: *Newsweek*, Feb. 23, 1976.)

Need I amplify this? Need anyone explain what this has to do with the Cold War, the domino theory, and Watergate?

I am also minorly aggrieved by New York publishers, about thirty of whom refused to look at this book. In *The Writer's Handbook*, a *Reader's Digest* editor explains that polls are used to determine what the public wants to read. He orders articles he judges in ascending order of acceptability: last, an article on economic conditions in the United States; next to last, on great fortunes in America; then, an economic analysis about Henry Ford; then "How I got rich," by Henry Ford; and first and foremost — "How *you* can get rich." Writers are advised to organize their thinking accordingly, on the grounds that everyone has these priorities.

Man continues to descend. He waves flags and prays to God to save his paltry soul, then turns around and knifes a poor people in Vietnam who has the guts to go against his fighters and bombers. That is the state of the world, exceptions like Scandinavia, with her excellent automobiles and jets, illustrating the morality which should be possible.

Our ignorant conservatives have done worse than can be stated. They have told Americans that the efficacious means are the shady ones, that there *are no others*, and that these have made America great. This is an ignorant view, whether or not its proponents use words like "anfractuosity." America had a unique opportunity to start from scratch, with resources so far beyond those of Europe and Scandinavia as to be all but unmeasurable. Now we must hope that our horizontal and vertical monopolies, our Krupps and their V-8 economy do not run out of oil.

Thomas Mann has written that to understand everything is to forgive everything. Well, that could be. The thought should sober all but the most hardened, however, that according to their own Christian religion, by supporting the war in Vietnam many special interests not only needlessly ruined countless lives this world, but their own in the next. I doubt that Christ will be complimentary on their love of country, their insistence on relying on physical force alone, and their economics.

The sex drive is not due to cultural learning. Cultural learning nevertheless determines that some lead lives of abstinence, such as the Russian monk, while others yield to every temptation. Perhaps this is also the relationship between the aggressive drive and cultural learning. The former provides only a predisposition and impetus, not the final form of the latter. Its force can be completely overridden, or carried to a ridiculous extreme. I believe Ashley Montagu himself would admit that the amount of time devoted to sex does pale into insignificance when compared to the time human beings devote to intra-specific competition. The impetus itself is beyond good and evil. It is the source of both. No one endorses it. A future generation will be enlightened on these matters as ours is not. That generation will more adequately answer Job's question as to why good men suffer while the less principled prosper and "grow mighty in power," to the detriment of everyone else.

will understand these things. They
em if they are to manage the new
will see to it that their youngsters
l *learn* from them. What did those
they will ask, and how often were
ow did the first lie — that a certain
piracy of Russian and Chinese com-
cond — that the United States was
cial system and benevolent leaders
se two lies make it necessary for men
agreements of 1954? How did these
decade-long intellectual dishonesty
nd civilian casualties? And how did
ple to continue with the hoax that
rast to others, was basically truthful?
mino theory valid? It is even possible
that future generations will derive one reason why most peoples
are too poor and unschooled to protect or limit their populations from Five Great Lies circulated in the rich and educated
countries.

The iced lies on which American foreign policy have been
based have a frozen-horse quality. They have filled Southeast
Asia with acrid fumes already. A few pungent vapors escaped
in America during the Watergate hearings. I cannot be irate
about the frozen mammoth in Siberia while this horse fills
my living room with putrefaction. As long as it can be kept
mostly frozen in a sick debate, demagogues can prosper by
selling aircraft to Arabs, Jews, and everyone else. But day by
day the horse thaws, and as it does it fills the world with its
terrible stench.

How should a teacher respond to that? Consider my position. Here I
had started a boy out in history, English, German, Russian — and, in an
attempt to tweak some patriotic thoughts from him, only aided him in
putting out the harshest judgment that ever a teacher heard from an
idealistic youth. I could not escape from him. Wherever and whatever
I taught, here was this stern misanthrope presenting me with new ver-
sions of the same essay. Whether I chose the Holy Roman Empire or

the extended adjectival modifier, I got the same response: Read *this*! Gratifying it was to note how I had influenced a student's development, an effort detectable in the shadow of my instruction in his writing. Still, misgivings outweighed approval and admiration for the work. The student still believed that ideas could be used to create a better world, a hope which I have unfortunately had to abandon. Writing my critique of Jerome's essays, I made use of his favorite authors, and flatter myself by believing that the following warnings and encouragement might also be of help to others who sympathize with his opinions.

American entrance into the Vietnam debacle could be described as an honest, if foolish mistake, though I admit that leaves one hard-put to find an explanation for the United States State Department's repeated condemnation of French bungling — nay, dull-witted belligerence and myopia — in Vietnam. A period of good intentions and honest simplicity was soon superseded by official awareness of faulty assessment of the conflict, and thus by more and more governmental secrecy, conscious hedging on every little thing. *Then* came lying, and finally continuance of the war with emphasis on heavy bombing, free-fire zones, body counts, and sophisticated firepower, on the grounds that withdrawal would be clumsy, might result in reprisals as bad as the air war, and *would* result in a loss of face which no American President could envision. Some special interests had a hand. The public had little to say.

Anthony Storr wrote: "The complexities of the circumstances which provoke war are such that no one man and no one viewpoint can possibly comprehend them all. Anyone who promises a solution to a problem so perennial is too arrogant to be trusted . . ." Historians of India may one day write that Gandhi should have abandoned his crusade for passive resistance and instead taught his people a few biological facts. Do Jerome's contemporaries appreciate the complexity of problem-solving? If not, one day an Eric Hoffer will blame a historical catastrophe on them and all other "men of words," just as Nietzsche was blamed for the rise of a Nazi party which would expurgate his books. Jerome and all like him should consider Lincoln's words addressed to them: "If there ever could be a proper time for mere catch arguments, that time surely is not now."

Nor has Jerome succeeded in analyzing the complexity of educational progress. Many of his thoughts are fine, but so quixotic! Illiteracy he defines as the inability or failure to read. But there is an even more serious kind of illiteracy: choosing journals and books which support one's own view and avoiding others. Some renowned personalities are practically illiterate as a result. How can *schools* combat a problem like that?

For the United States or any other country to improve schools, it would have to overcome the divorce of an academic elite from the man-on-the-street. Within universities this brand of polarization is mirrored in snobbish disputes between schools of education and other departments. If schools of education could settle their differences with scholars long enough to design a four- or six-year graduated history sequence to compare with four- and six-year wrestling sequences, the whole situation would be transformed. One should not hold one's breath until that happens.

As for quixotic solutions, I have one myself. That university study is restricted to high school graduates is one of the follies of our time. One cannot discuss *Macbeth* with children. They lack the necessary experience. Let us teach children the basic skills, and when it comes time for them to attend a university, let us permit them when possible to learn their parents' work. When they have mastered that, they can support their elders while the latter attend universities. The parents need a rest after raising children to near adulthood. They will be more interesting to have in class and will enjoy the experience more. While the parents study, their children will learn from their own example how human beings behave. They will not quite have time to ruin everything, however, for parents will write home with advice along with requests for money. When the parents have had their stint at the universities it will be their children's turn. Now all those subjects at which adolescents sniff will be relevant. Experienced students should, as Meg Greenfield says, learn more from a course in history than in Crisis of the Cities 211A.

Meanwhile, let the school organize a history program with the emphasis and care it devotes to football. Some of the teacher's problems with motivation will then begin to recede. Students sense immediately how important liberal arts are to a community, and that is the importance they attach to them. Both Dewey and his opponent Hutchins wanted the sequence, time, and effort devoted to humanities courses for everyone's benefit which Europeans reserve for a few, and Americans for a few star athletes. Instead, as Hutchins states in his famous *Great Conversation*, the educationists who so admired Dewey have foisted on generations of youth a theory of social adjustment he quite explicitly detested.

"Enlightened self-knowledge," "heightened consciousness level," "a renaissance of good reading habits" — everyone calls for educational progress, and what good does it do? Intellectual pursuits make the most wearisome occupations tolerable, which might be a good argument in favor of adult education. A fine idea, but it won't work.

Then again, I can only second many of Jerome's thoughts. He is not really a negative person, may I add. He still hunts, fishes, plays pool, and goes out with young ladies. He enjoys going home to the farm. I like to think of him as speaking for the better half of myself. He has not given up seeking applications for ideas — which was, after all, the best thing I could do to make the rocky road to tenure an easier one. He is right that one needn't choose between doing things right in graduated programs and education for all, any more than one need choose between basic drives and cultural factors in explaining human behavior. With a little selective cultural borrowing, American institutions could derive the best from the *Realschule*, where chemistry, physics, and biology are taught simultaneously in a six-year sequence, in addition to six years of history, foreign language, and other subjects — with compulsory school attendance for only half the day. A nation needn't choose between Pestalozzi's graduated instruction and social mobility, between social leveling and elitism, between athletics and learning.

One of the most depressing thoughts of every teacher must be that prosperous generations far in the future will not really learn from history, but will entertain themselves with troubles of the past. After the most difficult avoidable problems have been eliminated, from airplane accidents to overpopulation, how will anyone comprehend the level of civilization attained? Such people will be farther from us than we are from our grandparents. They will never understand what it was like to listen to Richard Nixon and William Buckley and to watch the Vietnam War. Books, even films, cannot carry the power of experience into the future. If I could see how knowledge could be passed from generation to generation, I would share Jerome's enthusiasm for education. I don't believe it can.

Colleges blew up like pressure cookers put on the stove with no escape valve. As a teacher I struggled against the rising pressure, and am struggling against the aftermath of the inevitable hemorrhage. That the destruction of students' equilibrium was messy has been observed in great detail as the decay of morality — a problem not worth discussing if our purpose is to get to the bottom of the trouble: the heat applied.

Some can live along happily while millions of lives are wrecked by man's ignorance. Others cannot, especially those not yet hardened to the behavior of the human race. If Jerome has dedicated his part of this book to the leadership which wound down the war, I dedicate my part to the students hurt in demonstrations.

If Jerome's writing is vituperative, it expresses the frustration of innumerable students seeking direction — and no doubt of many adults who feel themselves disenfranchised. What can I tell them? Can I disappoint them again? Well, Jerome wrote an essay called "Peace with Honor," and showed that there was no peace with honor. He wrote an essay on healthy debate, and showed that the debate is not at all healthy. So the reader will be prepared for my admission that I do not have the last word to what he has written either.

One does not blame people because they do not say to themselves, as my personal model Schliemann did, that they will take ten or twenty years to perfect their knowledge and then tackle an apparently hopeless task in some corporation. It is possible, though, to remind today's youth that some of them will enter politics, some business, some the work force, some medicine, others education, and others the military, and that Schliemann's conception of dedication would not harm them if they are serious about change. Let them beware of false hedonism and take consolation in the words of Adalbert Stifter: "There is no great and no small life work."

Unfortunately, however, general enlightenment will have to wait for another era. For now even a Frenchman can say, "If Americans did in fact bomb the ARVN, I'm sure they will have some good reason for it." And a German can declare, "If Americans are so rich, why aren't they smart?"

Jerome's solutions may be quixotic, but that is not his fault. Then, too, perhaps he will sway a few minds. Perhaps the editors of *Reader's Digest* could see their way to popularize the views of someone besides Melvin Laird and his ilk, who (though they dimly understand the war) do not appreciate that the best friend of the communist cause in Southeast Asia was the United States military. That would be something.

Jerome will join fine company in failure. Georg Kaiser wrote the epitaph of a generation of writers, none of whom were understood during their lifetime: "Our voice could have roused the desert. Men were deaf." Dürrenmatt consoles, "Every attempt by an individual to solve problems which concern everyone must fail . . . Problems which concern everyone can only be solved by everyone." And Stifter's thought is one I occasionally repeat to myself as a schoolteacher: There is no small and no great life work. Like so many of Jerome's quotes, this one may not be entirely *true*, but it helps.

Beware of easy knowledge, fast solutions, generalizations before detail. If one has nothing to meditate on, how will one meditate? The youth of today want their answers too fast and too easy. Remember what Bronowski said on the "Ascent of Man": Please leave room for the unexpected, and for that ever so small possibility that you may be wrong. Jerome and I have searched for the last word and come up empty-handed.

Mark Twain nonetheless urged everyone to continue searching and re-correcting his views:

Who are the thousand — that is to say, who are "the country"? In a monarchy, the king and his family are the country; in a republic, it is the common voice of the people. Each of you, for himself, by himself, and on his own responsibility, must speak. And it is a solemn responsibility, not lightly to be flung aside at the bullying of the pulpit, the press, government, or the empty catch-phrases of politicians. Each

MARCH 1974

Despite the Kissinger-Tho communique of June 13, 1973, calling anew for the full implementation of the ceasefire and the political provisions of the Paris accord, reporters in Vietnam found that Saigon's commanders had received no ceasefire orders.

The *New York Times* has reported $813 million in U.S. military aid being sent to Thieu in fiscal 1974, and Pentagon plans for $1 billion more thereafter to enlarge and modernize Saigon's forces. Some 8,000 "civilian" advisers and technicians have been provided

Newsweek, October 7, 1974

relief workers are bitter. In the town of El Progresso, an exhausted Peace Corps worker slumped down on the grass. "Planes are coming in from all over the world, and the military is stashing everything away in their warehouses," he exploded. "We've seen nothing, nothing at all, and we are faced with outbreaks of typhoid, malaria and measles." An American volunteer doctor was more philosophical. "Once the army has filled its *bodegas* [warehouses] the people who need the relief will get what is left. That's better than nothing."

Islam said an average of 16,500 people had died every week for the past six weeks in Bangladesh.

TIME, SEPTEMBER 30, 1974

Question: "Under what international law do we have a right to attempt to destabilize the constitutionally elected government of another country?"
Answer: "I am not going to pass judgment on whether it is permitted or authorized under international law. It is a recognized fact that historically as well as presently, such actions are taken in the best interest of the countries involved."

That blunt response by President Gerald Ford at his press conference last

Until last week, members of both the Nixon and Ford Administrations had flatly denied that the U.S. had been involved in undermining Allende's regime. They continue to insist that the CIA was not responsible for the 1973 coup that left Allende dead and a repressive right-wing junta in his place.

Congressmen were outraged by the news that they had once again been misled by the Executive Branch.

Newsweek, January 13, 1975

A jury of twelve ordinary Americans affirmed in law last week what events had long since made perfectly clear: that Richard Nixon's Presidency was the most pervasively corrupt in U.S. history.

TIME, DECEMBER 23, 1974

VIET NAM

Fighting for the Leopard Spots

With good reason, some gloomy citizens in Saigon are by now convinced that the war in South Viet Nam will never end. Last week fighting between Communist and government troops reached its greatest intensity since the ineffective cease-fire, signed nearly two years ago. By week's end the South Vietnamese army (ARVN) had suffered 706 killed and 2,758 wounded; Saigon officials claim to have killed more than 3,600 of their enemies.

Most of the fighting was centered in the heavily populated and agricultur-

must for himself decide what is right and what is wrong, and which course is patriotic and which isn't. You cannot shirk this and be a man."

My student positively forbade me to cross the 100-page mark. In recompense for his cavalier treatment of our media, I will therefore, in the absence of a conclusion, allow the media to have the last word. Truth, *the* truth, the last word is everywhere, for those who can extract it and only for those.

April 30, 1975

Vietnam war over; Saigon surrenders

By GEORGE ESPER
Associated Press Writer
SAIGON—The Saigon government surrendered unconditionally to the Viet Cong today, ending 30 years of warfare.

The Last Word